moves from a vivid personal awareness of being forgiven to the power to serve others as an agent of reconciliation; and how a life centered in Christ gives freedom from the trivial and provides a disciplined focus amid the confusion and distraction of our times.

This is more than a practical handbook for Christian living. It is also a stirring call to new discipleship for all men who are dissatisfied with the shallowness of token belief and routine observance.

THE AUTHOR: Robert Raines's first book, NEW LIFE IN THE CHURCH, has been widely acclaimed by both clergy and laymen. He is minister of the First Methodist Church, Germantown, Pa., a pastorate to which he was called following distinguished and creative service at Aldersgate Methodist Church in Cleveland.

Reshaping the Christian Life

Robert A. Raines

Reshaping
the Christian Life

HARPER & ROW, PUBLISHERS

New York, Evanston, and London

Grateful acknowledgment is made to Holt, Rinehart and Winston, Inc., for permission to quote "The Gift Outright" from *Complete Poems of Robert Frost,* copyright 1942 by Robert Frost; to the Epworth Press for permission to quote "The Manse" from *Obiter Scripta* by William Russell Maltby; and to Harcourt, Brace & World, Inc., for permission to quote from "The Hollow Men" and "The Cocktail Party" from *Complete Poems and Plays,* copyright 1952 by T. S. Eliot.

FIRST EDITION

LIBRARY OF CONGRESS CATALOG CARD NUMBER: 64-15954

D-O

For Peggy

Contents

Preface

This book has been written over a period of two years, years which have marked a transition in my ministry. My thought and concern have shifted somewhat in emphasis from the life together of Christians to Christian mission in the world. Coincidental with this movement of thought was my move from a suburban parish to an urban one.

The book therefore expresses something of the uncertainty and groping of these years. As Robert Spike has commented, ours is an "exodus" time, in which we remember where we have been but are not quite sure where we are going. We are on the way in the wilderness and it is a way of venture, risk, and anticipation. The whole church is in a time of uneasy travail, which we may hope is the anguish implicit in creation.

I have tried to portray from inside of conventional congregational life what the coming reformation means for the ordinary church and the ordinary Christian. The book is necessarily a kind of personal documentary of the two congregations I have served and the Christian people I have known. While the inadequacies of the book are wholly my own, its value, if any, belongs entirely

to the Church of Jesus Christ, from which all that is real in my
own faith derives, and to which all that is useful in this book is
gratefully offered.

I would like to express gratitude to those whose thought, work,
kindness, and encouragement have helped me to write the book.
Frank Elliott, my kind friend and editor at Harper & Row, first
urged me to write such a book, endured with me as it underwent
considerable change of scope and direction, and encouraged me
at every turn. Kenneth W. Conners made valuable suggestions
for improving the manuscript and gave much encouragement.
Virginia Hamilton has generously given scores of hours to typing
and retyping the manuscript. Her skill, humor, and constant
good nature helped me immeasurably. Mr. and Mrs. Edward
Hutchison kindly made available to me their farmhouse, where
part of the book was written. Theodore W. Loder, my colleague
in the ministry, has graciously borne burdens of time and pressure
with me and for me while the writing was in process. My wife
Peggy, over two summers and on many "ministerial Mondays,"
has forgone family fellowship so that I might go off by myself and
work on the book. Her encouragement and confidence have been
the source of power to keep me at it until it was done.

Except where otherwise noted, Scripture quotations are from
the Revised Standard Version of the Bible.

Philadelphia, Pennsylvania   ROBERT A. RAINES
January, 1964

Reshaping the Christian Life

Chapter 1

The Shape of Christ

For my children you are, and I am in travail with
you over again until you take the shape of Christ.
                    Galatians 4:19 NEB

Recently I found myself one member of a panel of three persons discussing the nature and mission of the church. It happened that I sat in the middle, between a representative of the Church of the Saviour in Washington, D.C.,[1] and the minister of Judson Memorial Church of Greenwich Village, New York. The Church of the Saviour is a community of Christians who have grown through commitment, discipline, and mission into an extraordinarily deep fellowship. They are impressive chiefly because of what they *are*—their quality of being. The Judson Church is a community of Christians who have gone redemptively into the nightclubs, apartments, and cultural world of their neighborhood to be salt, light, and leaven. They are impressive because of what they *do*—their quality of doing. As the conversation proceeded, it struck me how strangely appropriate it was that I, a representative of the "conventional" parish church today, should be seated between representatives of two such unconventional Christian congregations. I felt both personally and representatively judged by the quality of *being* embodied in the Church of the Saviour and the quality of *doing* embodied in the Judson Church. In the light of their witness, the darkness of the being and the doing—the life together and the mission—of the conventional church became painfully clear. In this connection Paul's word to the Galatian Christians of the first century speaks to our condition in the mid-twentieth century: "For my children you are, and I am in travail with you over again until you take the shape of Christ."

The church must be reshaped. We can see now that the church needs more than inner renewal within traditional patterns. The wine of new life makes new wineskins necessary. Nothing less than transformation and reshaping will enable the church to be reborn into the kind of being and doing that will be adequate for God's purpose in our day. We are being called to discover new shapes of life together in the church and new shapes of mission in the world.

1. *The church is hollow in its life together.* There is in our fellowship a colorless insipidity and an absence of unique relationship. The salt has lost its savor, the light grows dim in the dark world, the leaven appears lost in the lump, and the sheep look very much like the wolves. If Jesus' question to the first disciples were put to us, ". . . what is there extraordinary about . . . [your behavior]?" (Matt. 5:47, NEB), we should have to answer, "Nothing." If our discipleship is to be known in the world by the quality of our love for one another (John 13:35), can we wonder that, to a world walking in shadowed valleys, the church does not look like a city set on a hill? Florence Allshorn writes,

People outside Christianity look at our little Christian groups, our parish churches, our Christian schools, colleges, societies, and fail to see them shining out like light in dark places. Christian committees, diocesan councils, missionary bodies, all these should be centers of light, of the Spirit—and so often they are not. Instead of "How these Christians love one another," we hear, "I never go near church societies or parish organizations, there is so much gossip and rivalry."[2]

Increasing numbers of perceptive and sensitive people, both inside and outside the church, are becoming disillusioned with it. This was underlined for me in a letter from friends who had moved to another city and were trying to find a new church. Granting that the letter gives us something of a caricature, but remembering that a caricature is only an exaggeration of reality, let us look for a shadow of our own churches cast herein. The person writes,

Horrible as I have always thought the practice of "church shopping" to be, that is precisely what we have been doing. Our first couple of Sundays here we went to the big church in town. At this church we heard passable sermons, but closer acquaintance with the minister and congregation quickly disillusioned us. We noted the subject for a men's fellowship meeting as "How to Be a Success in Business." We learned from *the* president of *the* bank in town that this church is the most acceptable socially. But what really finished off our interest in it was the minister himself. He came here to call one day, and I have seldom met a less spiritual "spiritual" leader. His major church concerns seemed to be with *things*, such as the new organ and carillon some anonymous benefactor had provided, to the tune of $60,000— as he proudly informed me. He didn't offer to pray with me, and his invitation to Christian discipleship was a suggestion that he and his wife take us some night to the City Club for dinner, this being the most exclusive club in town, where he is a member.

In the hour of the church's institutional success, its spiritual failure is being exposed. In the 1950's hungry men and women flocked into the churches seeking new life and were often handed, instead, old programs. They discovered that they could become and remain lost just as easily in the church as in the community service club, and far more poignantly. Many nibbled at the edges of the crust but never found the bread of life. So in the 1960's we see signs of the ebb of this surging hope, as people drift out of the church, disillusioned by the discovery that the church did not deliver on its promise of new life in Christ.

As clergy and laymen concerned about the church, we rightly begin to ask ourselves, "Are we in the ranks of those unspiritual

'spiritual' leaders, more interested in things than theology, in property than prayer, more concerned to grow in numbers than to grow in grace?" Have we become confused about the real nature of the church? The letter quoted above speaks of a city church, with an impressive structure and budget, whose annual reports must look very successful—as we would say, one of our great churches. What is a "great" church? I wince when I hear ecclesiastical leaders referring to this or that church as "great," because they almost always speak of churches with a thousand members or more, churches with imposing buildings and budgets. Greatness is defined in secular terms. But the truly great church of all time was a loosely organized collection of lower-class people (I Cor. 1:26-31) who met in one another's homes for worship, prayer, study, and fellowship together. They had no buildings, no relish for ecclesiastical titles or privilege; there was not a D.D. among them. They could not have cared less about worldly power or status. They had found life in Jesus Christ! The mark of greatness in any community that calls itself the church of Jesus Christ, the mark that determines whether in fact this community *is* the church of Christ, is the presence of the risen Christ calling people into the *koinonia*, transforming persons and fashioning the congregation into the living shape of Christ. The hollowness of our life together must be filled by the fullness of Christ taking shape among us.

The church is irrelevant in its mission. There have been a number of books issued lately, generally written by sociologists, documenting the irrelevance of the church in the modern world.[3] C. Wright Mills put it as well as anyone: "As a social and personal force, religion has become a dependent variable: It does not set forth new modes of conduct and sensibility; it imitates . . . . It has become less a revitalization of the spirit in permanent tension with the world than a respectable distraction from the sourness of life."[4] A vivid picture of the irrelevant stance of the church in the world appeared on the front page of *The New York Times* on Monday, April 15, 1963. It showed three well-dressed and obviously well-mannered Negroes quietly descending the steps of the Sixth Avenue Presbyterian Church in Birmingham, Alabama, where they had just been refused entrance for Easter Sunday worship. Behind them three elders of the church stood, like stone pillars, guarding the closed doors of the church. In a world swept by the power of God along the way of desegregation and racial justice, eleven o'clock Sunday morning remains the most segregated hour of American life— despite recent awakening to the crisis in many parts of the church. Thus we in the church are judged by God, and by many others, as standing in the way of God's reconciling work in the world.

It is the mission of the church to participate in God's mission in and to the world—a mission of reconciliation (II Cor. 5:16-20). This means that the church must be informed about the significant problems, issues, and human needs of its world and in both congregational and personal life become responsibly involved in dealing redemptively with them. J. H. Oldham writes,

There is only one place at which a genuine renewal of the life of the Church can take place, namely, at the point at which its mission of transforming the world is being fulfilled. The only real renewal is a healing and saving manifestation of the power of love in open and courageous encounter with the world. The Church is not a separate sphere of existing reality, distinct from the natural world and history; it is a new dimension of reality penetrating these realms and transforming them. The essential life of the Church is an unrestricted energy of freely working love within the world. As minister of the forgiving and healing love of God, the Church has to enter into the whole structure of society and mingle with the sinfulness of secular life. It is only in the place where men sin that they can be redeemed. The new life in Christ has its reality, its center, its manifestation, not in any separate religious sphere, but in the life of every-day, in the context of the natural world and history, in every act which the Christian performs in faith.[5]

New shapes of mission both for congregations and for individuals must be found whereby the church can once again take the shape of Christ in the world for which He died.

2. *The church can be reshaped.* Some of the most prophetic churchmen of our day have little hope for the reshaping of the church. They point to the overwhelming institutionalism of the typical congregation, the opaque barriers to deep personal relationships, the fragmenting busyness. They speak of the vested-interest conservatism of both ecclesiastical and lay leadership, and the rigidity of congregational and denominational structures. They say that only by starting outside conventional denominational and parochial structures is there sufficient freedom to experiment, to learn by trial and error what the Spirit would have us be and do in our time. We must listen to these spokesmen, recognize them as bearers of the Spirit, and be grateful for the courageous ventures they are making, and for all that we are learning from them. They are the frontier crossers of our day, the pilgrims, the pioneers. It is they who will show us, if we are faithful, where the Spirit is leading the whole church.

Nevertheless, I dare to believe there is hope for the reshaping of congregational and personal life within conventional structures. If I did not, I would leave the parish ministry. I believe the church can be reshaped because of what may be termed the theological, sociological, and biblical perspectives.

a. *The theological perspective.* God is a God who brings down and raises up, a God who destroys and builds again. He is a judging God whose judgment is not punitive but redemptive. He is a God whose sovereign grace leads men to repent and be transformed. He is a God who is always doing a new thing, who is ever shaping and reshaping His people. He is a God whose Spirit moved over the void in the event of creation and throughout history, unto our own time, continues to move over the cosmos in new creation. We believe in this God whose Spirit is ever creating and renewing the church of Jesus Christ. Reformation is the constant theme of church history. W. A. Visser 't Hooft writes,

If we would only watch more carefully the signs of the times, especially of our own times, we would never cease to wonder at this astonishing power of renewal which is given to the Church, whenever and wherever it accepts to be renewed. Calvin's word that the story of the Church is a story of many resurrections, is true, and its truth ought to colour and dominate our whole thinking about the present and future of the Church. . . . the Church learns all through its history that "Though our outer nature is wasting away, our inner nature is being renewed every day" (II Cor. 4:16).[6]

The reformation of the church is a continuing work of the Holy Spirit. The new Spirit-impelled movements give their particular gift, make their unique witness, and eventually lose their lives in the body of the whole church that the life of the whole church may be saved. The whole church, the church universal, has been, is now, and ever shall be the bearer of the gospel.

b. *The sociological perspective.* Whether present church structures are impervious to renewal or not, there does seem often to be an unfortunate perversity about contemporary discussion of the issue. The "old structure" party is defensive; the "new structure" party is offensive. We must not let the heat of the dialogue divert us from the light of truth emerging from it. The threefold truth is that some structure is *necessary*, that structures must *change*, and that new structures are *begotten*, not made.

Structure—institutional form—is necessary for communication. Jesus was "revealed in human shape" (Phil. 2:8, NEB), the Word became flesh, and the treasure was lodged in earthen vessels. Human shape, flesh, and earthen vessel are neither expendable nor harmful; they are vehicles for the incarnation of the presence of God among us. Therefore, we will always need some structures to express and embody our life and work as the church of Jesus Christ. We cannot get away from structure, nor do we will to. Structure comes to us by the grace of creation.

But structures need constantly to be changing. James M. Gustafson writes,

Because it is a *human community* the Church can make Christ present to me. Its social adaptiveness is a strength rather than a weakness, a good rather than an evil. It must find the political forms, patterns of interpretation, and liturgies through which Christ can make Himself present to the disinherited Negroes and Puerto Ricans of Manhattan, the Hindu Tamils of Ceylon, the dying aristocracy of Western Europe, and the people of Eastern Europe under Soviet domination. Failure to adapt means failure in its mission. It found patterns effective for its mission among the serfs of medieval Christendom and the *bourgeoisie* of the mercantile age; it must find them for the rising nationalists of Africa and Asia in our century. It has defined its beliefs in relation to Platonism through Augustine and the Church Fathers, to Aristotelianism through St. Thomas, to existentialism through Bultmann; it must define them in relation to logical analysis through theologians of our decade. . . . The Church is a chameleon. It finds colors that fit it into various environments. It continues, yet changes; this is the value of its social nature. Yet it stands always under the order and judgment of God to whom it professes loyalty and in whom it believes. It is a human community, with a particular vocation, purpose, and power.[7]

So the church must always live in the tension of the old order yielding place to the new, holding fast to that which is good and reaching out to that which is better.

New structures are begotten, not made. We do not achieve new forms, we receive them. God gives both the new wine and the new wineskins, in His own time and way. It is not by our ingenuity that the reformation comes but by our obedient perception and reception of the new shapes God is preparing. There is, then, a paradoxical urgency and nonchalance about our waiting upon the Lord. We know *Who* is coming, but we do not know *what* is coming. And the question is, will we recognize Him when we see Him revealed in human shape? In a time of reformation we are like the painter in the moment of new creation described by James Brooks:

It is a paradoxical situation. There is a moment when you know things are happening, but can't predict them. The problem is that recognition is in terms of memory, like a Matisse shape or a Picasso shape. You want your own shapes, but since you have never seen them before, you have to feel them after they are there.[8]

This is our predicament until we take the shape of Christ.

c. *The biblical perspective.* Paul evidently believed that the seriously divided and misguided congregations of Galatia could yet take the shape of Christ. Even more suggestive are his letters to the Corinthian Church. There was much trouble in that congregation—personal dissension, partisan division, doctrinal confusion, moral failure. As we read about it we find ourselves nodding and saying, "Yes, this is the church I know in my own experience. Here are people struggling and groping just the way the people of our church seem to be doing." But when we come to the third chapter of Paul's second letter to the Corinthians we are surprised and somewhat shocked. He writes to this Corinthian congregation, "You yourselves are our letter of recommendation, written on your hearts, to be known and read by all men; and you show that you are a letter from Christ delivered by us, written not with ink but with the Spirit of the living God, not on tablets of stone but on tablets of human hearts" (II Cor. 3:2-3).

That congregation—a letter from Christ? To be known and read by all men? Was Paul actually saying to them that they, with all of their failure and weakness, were even so a genuine letter from Christ to the world of Corinth? He was saying just that, and in those words we can find real hope for our own situation.

Every Christian congregation is a "letter from Christ" to its own community. The letter may be all but unreadable and may, in fact, need to be rewritten by the Spirit. But the gospel truth is that it *is* a communication from Christ. Paul did not say, "You should be a letter," or "You must become a letter," but "You *are* a letter from Christ." Every local congregation, no matter how shallow its life together or how stultified its mission, has buried within it the treasure of Christ's presence. The *koinonia* may be hidden and dormant, but it can be uncovered and resurrected.

Every clergyman and layman is called to dig for the treasure hidden in the earthen vessel of his own congregation. One of the things we discover as we dig is that there is more evidence of the treasure than we had at first suspected. For here and there in the congregation we come across great Christians of whom the world never hears, ordinary men and women become extra-ordinary by the power of Christ in the fellowship. Christ is ever revealing a fresh facet of Himself in the most unlikely persons among us. He shows forth His compassion in this person, His humility in that one, His indignation in another, His peace in one, and His anguish in the same one. Our knowledge and love of Christ deepen as we meet Him in the faces and hearts of His people.

3. *The church is being reshaped.* One of the most helpful books I have read tells the story of Florence Allshorn and the missionary renewal center she inspired in England. A missionary herself, she saw how the idealistic, zealous young missionaries became dis-couraged in their first tour of duty in the mission field. She felt called to create a community of healing and restoration for such missionaries. She speaks of the motivation for establishing St. Julian's:

> In the past the emphasis for those trying to live a more dedicated Christian life had been on the need for an unusual effort to alter situations single-handed. Now the leading of the Spirit seemed to be that the witness of living together a truly Christian life was more needed than solitary greatness.[9]

Not solitary greatness but the witness of living together a truly Christian life. I was struck when I read these words. For almost every creative Christian venture of our time, inside or outside the conventional structures, has been a search for vital life together in Christ, for Christian community. One thinks of the Iona Community in Scotland, the Evangelical Academies of Germany, the Taizé Community in France, the East Harlem Protestant Parish and other ecumenical inner-city parishes, the house-church movement in Leeds, England, Koinonia Farm in Georgia, the Faith and Life Community at the University of Texas in Austin, the widespread retreat movement, and other similar ventures. Most of these arose after the Second World

War without special respect to geography, locale, or denomination. No one organized this universal longing to recover the corporate life and mission of the church. It is the work of the Spirit calling us to belong to Christ and to one another in a life together that takes the shape of Christ in the world.

It is widely agreed that such corporate witness must come into being in the world where people live and work and fight and play—not in the cloister or chapel. For in our time the world is not going to come and search in the cloister or chapel. The world will be moved by the church only when it sees something different and extraordinary in our presence in daily life. Florence Allshorn tells us "of a young R.A.F. pilot, who said to a Christian, 'Don't try to help me or preach to me, or tell me what I ought to think yet. Don't work for my salvation, show me yours, show me it is possible, and the knowledge that something works will give me courage. . . .' "[10] The need is to create here and there in the desert of modern industrial society oases of *koinonia*, small groups of living, working Christians, where the world can see the greenness of new life springing up and taste the water of life, places where Christ may show Himself to the outsider.

This witness, whenever and wherever possible, will be corporate. For the individual Christian standing alone in the factory, corporation, college, city, or other modern mission field of whatever nature is often unable to be an effective witness. The Christian will bind himself to one or two others in the structures of common life and seek to provide, out there in the world, a body where Christ may take shape, the Christ who promised that He would be present when two or three gather in His name and Spirit. A German theologian said in conversation recently, "Today (unlike the time of the Reformation) the problem is not how to find a gracious God, but how to find a gracious neighbor." Most men in the modern world will discover the gracious God only in and through gracious neighbors, creating a veritable neighborhood of grace in the world. It is our task to create such communities of grace in every corner and sector of modern life, so that a world seeking community can find it in Christ. The Holy Spirit is in very truth moving upon us, in a time of new creation, out of whose travail we may hope to take the shape of Christ.

When a man stands outside a great cathedral looking at the stained-glass windows he may see merely the bare, meaningless outlines of the glass. There may be no color or significance. But when he goes inside the cathedral and looks up at the windows, now brilliant with the sunlight and sparkling with color, he sees them transfigured. The light unveils the figures and discloses their features. The story carved in glass begins to live, and its glory is revealed.

As we enter the portals of the living church, we shall look for glory but not without suffering, for joy but not without cost, for resurrection but not without death. The glory will come only by the agony of rebirth. The joy will come only out of the cost of our unconditional commitment to Christ and to one another. The resurrection together will come only as we die to ourselves. This is no individual quest. It is the corporate pilgrimage of those who are willing to be baptized into the family of Christ and equipped for mission as the army of the Lord.

The chapters that follow are an effort to discern some outlines of an emerging shape in the life of the corporate fellowship (Part I) and in the spiritual career of the individual believer (Part II). The reader will swiftly become aware, however, that this division is at best a convenient arrangement for treating realities that are inextricably bound together in life. Individual and community must grow together or the growth of either will be stunted. Within each Part, my attempt has been to describe a movement from roots to flowering, a direction from inward reception to outward mission, from being to doing. But even this pattern must be inconsistent to reflect the actualities of Christian living. Many of the illustrative examples are drawn from my own experience in the parish, for it is that experience that has most inspired and nourished my work and the reflections I have set down. Aware of the limitations of this experience and the partiality of the suggestion offered, I dare to hope this book may contribute to an ongoing reformation whose course and form cannot be predicted.

In a time when the world searches for community and the church longs for reformation, we shall remember that "There's a divinity that shapes our ends, Rough-hew them how we will . . . ,"[11] a divinity that would mold us into the shape of Christ.

PART I. Reshaping the Church

Chapter 2

The Family of Christ

> Whoever does the will of God is my brother, and
> sister, and mother.
>
> > Mark 3:35

The church is the family of Christ. Jesus spoke of His disciples
as His brothers and sisters (Mark 3:35), called them to an al-
legiance higher than blood-tie loyalty (Luke 14:26), and promised them new brothers and sisters in the fellowship of His
followers (Mark 10:30). There are three constitutive elements
that characterize our participation in the family of Christ.

First, *we belong to Christ by belonging to each other*. Because
we belong to Christ, we also belong to each other. He who has
chosen us also chooses those who are our brothers and sisters.
We have no choice in the matter. Some of our brothers we may
like; others we may dislike. But they belong to us and we belong
to them in either case. Because we are involved with Him, we
are involved with them. And the reverse is also true: through
them we move closer to Him. We cannot be loyal to Him without being loyal to them. We cannot deny them without deny-
ing Him. We might wish to avoid this horizontal belonging and
cling only to Him. But we cannot do so. We belong to Christ
only by belonging to each other.

A perceptive executive and his wife found themselves in a

Bible study group composed of a broad diversity of people, some of immediate interest to them and some of little. In the course of their months of study and discussion together, surprising relationships developed among the members who at first had had so little in common. The executive described the group experience in these words:

> In our group one couple didn't seem to fit in at first. They didn't participate much. The wife very seldom spoke, and when the husband did, the rest of us were amused because things seemed so clear and simple to him, whereas the rest of us were debating and analyzing the complexities of Biblical passages. My wife and I discussed the matter on the way home one night, and concluded that it was because he wasn't very well educated. I am sure we were somewhat condescending. We did notice, however, that when this man prayed, he was much more at home than most of us in the group. He enjoyed something we didn't have—a deep and abiding faith in God. We talked about God; he knew God. He had the kind of rapport with God which the rest of us wanted and were seeking. Not long ago, this man lost his wife. She was twenty-eight years old and had suffered from a heart condition for many years. When we visited him at the funeral home and saw his complete acceptance of what had happened with no streak of bitterness, I no longer saw his dirty fingernails or poor grooming, or noticed his grammatical errors. If ever in all of my life I have seen a true reflection of Christ, I saw it in that man. My wife and I were humbled by his strength and stature. I bow to that man. From the witness of his life I know Christ a little better.

It is a strange and marvelous fact that in the family of Christ we give and receive gifts of Christ's grace far beyond our own intention or expectation. Often Christ becomes most real to us in one of those whom we least expected to be a vehicle of His presence. The eye and the hand do need each other, for they are members of the same living body. But it is only as we acknowledge one another as brothers that we discover Him who called us into brotherhood. He comes to us where two or three are bound together in His name, and teaches us to love one another as He has loved us.

Second, *we learn Christ's love by learning to love each other*. Members of a family have to struggle to learn to love one another. When any human association goes deep and involves real interdependence, the pressures and tensions become severe. We discover that living in family peace does not come easily. In the main it is not something we achieve through such struggle, but rather something we receive. It is a gift given by the God of Peace. A bridge club or a community social group may have very little friction in its common life because very little is at stake and little personal commitment is required. One comes into and can go out of such a group with no loss of anything vital to his personal identity and fulfillment. But in the family of Christ we are all bound together unconditionally. Our very belonging is a commitment to learn to love one another as He loves us. This kind of relationship, if it is not to break apart from the conflicting tensions, calls for more than surface smiles and the exchange of clever stories and confidences. It requires the humility to accept correction and guidance from a brother in Christ, the pain of real growth. We must forgive even those who do not forgive us; we must bear and forbear even with those (especially with those) who do not respond in kind.

Florence Allshorn describes the common experience of those who seek to learn Christ's love by the struggle to love each other:

Every one, we suppose, builds up his or her life with some picture of himself. Some people are a lot like the picture they build, some are a little like it, and some not at all. But no one *knows* himself until the picture is challenged and perhaps broken altogether. It was really a terrible time, this breaking up of the pictures we had each made for ourselves. At times it seemed intolerable. We knew hate, and malice, and that dreadful desire to hit back hard if we had been hurt. We found things buried deep in ourselves which were really shocking. Such deep resentment perhaps that one knew one could not forgive, and yet saying every day the Lord's Prayer. There was the misery caused by pride that refused to give in, and yet we chose that misery rather than give in . . . . We were new to this, and we had no pattern. It was the carving out of the pattern that was the grimmest part.[1]

Carving out the pattern is always the grimmest part. It is costly to be carved into the shape of Christ. There is the humiliation of discovering our own sin, and of knowing that we need one another. There is the mutual covenant which can release us only by binding us together. There is the risk of entrusting ourselves to one another, the risk of being hurt, misunderstood, or ignored.

We know there is no peace, whatever kind of façade is put on, for people who somewhere inside themselves have a fear of being known. They must break through this fear, no matter at what cost, if they are going to have any message for this generation.[2]

It takes great courage to love and be loved like this. Love is the capacity to reveal yourself to another, and to let another reveal himself to you. It is a new kind of seeing. Love is the capacity to be reconciled to another, and to let another be reconciled to you. It is a new kind of being. God makes it possible for us to love one another because He first loved us. He has revealed Himself to us in Christ and reconciled us to Himself through Christ. We learn Christ's love by learning to love one another and thus release His gracious gifts in one another.

Third, *the family of Christ is a ministering community*. We make a glorious discovery in the family of Christ. We find that we are not merged into a colorless uniformity in which each loses his individuality in some kind of collective entity. But, as Paul writes, "individually grace is given to us in different ways out of the rich diversity of Christ's giving" (Eph. 4:7, Phillips). It is in the family of Christ that each person emerges in freedom to be himself and to give his own unique gift to the fellowship. It is in the family that Christ liberates the true self of a man, so that what appears to the outsider as mundane is revealed to the brother as truly of heaven. The family of Christ is a ministering community.

One evening my wife and I were in the Coffee House of the Church of the Saviour in Washington, D.C.[3] Among the members of the church we met that night was an English woman, a sensitive person, acutely aware of suffering in others because of her own particular sorrow. She told us about herself, and how she heard about this church, how she came timidly to worship and was welcomed into its family life together. As she talked quietly and gladly of her new family, we felt a deep kinship with her after less than an hour's conversation. It was that strange recognition which is granted to us now and again when Christ is present in our midst, the awareness that those who have appeared to us as strangers are, in truth, members of our own family. A few weeks later we received a letter from her. She wrote, "Just recently I have been working in the church, in our art shop, enameling on copper plates. The articles have been sold at the Coffee House. It was fun to give the workshop a try, and I felt a decided force behind me in that everyone else had faith in my creative ability, except me!"

Here is the story, in miniature, of Christ's church wherever it is truly His family. This woman's personal creative gifts were released in the fellowship of those who had unbounded confidence in God's grace to work in her. In the ministering community she was enabled to take her part in Christ's work. Christ's family is the truly charismatic community where the personhood of each is set free to enrich the whole fellowship. We are not solitary saints but a company of sinners-being-made-saints. We are not individual flickering candles of faith but the focused light and warmth of a hearth fire. We are bound together in a healing, transforming, liberating fellowship, in which all the variety of our gifts contributes to a marvelous richness, and all our weakness provides a medium for the manifestation of Christ's power. He is above all, and through all, and in all. He releases the gifts of ministry.

Now, what in fact does all this have to do with the church as we know it in our own experience? One thing is clear. The church is not this kind of beloved family for most of its members. Instead of being offered the rich fulfillment of belonging to one another in Christ, church people are typically invited into the

sort of fellowship described in a newsletter from a highly "successful" church on the west coast: "The choir's 'Fun Night'
Wednesday, August 30th, brings a delightful summer of church
activities to a climax closing. This shall have been the busiest
summer thus far our church has had. Beach-parties, work-days,
car washes, pot-lucks, fun-nights, outings at the Bowl, theatre
and ball-park have added up to enriching the lives of hundreds."
Togetherness, American style, is not to be confused with participation in the family of Christ.

Many church members do not understand that they are called
to belong to Christ by belonging to their fellow members. They
believe that belonging to a church means that their spiritual
needs will now be taken care of, not that they will begin to take
care of the spiritual needs of others. They expect to be served,
not to serve. And woe betide the minister who hasn't dropped
in to call recently! Characteristically, such people feel that they
pay the clergyman to *be* the minister and regard themselves as
consumers of his ministry. They are the religious market; he is
the salesman. They are the patients; he is the doctor. They are
the public; he is the politician. And too often their expectations
are realized. The church becomes a voluntaristic society of individuals related to a clergyman instead of a community of
persons bound together in the mutual ministry of Christ's love.

How can the conventional congregation in our time become a
family of Christ? Sunday worship alone is inadequate. It is clear
that those who do not even know one another's names among
the scores of hundreds of worshipers on a Sunday morning can
scarcely belong to each other in any personal sense. No matter
how inspirational a service of worship may be, it simply is not in
itself the context in which people can become related to one
another as brothers and sisters in Christ. For many, worship is
largely a spectator experience that is almost anonymously carried
on for years without significant personal involvement in life
together with other Christians.

Preaching alone is inadequate. However powerful and brilliant preaching may be, it cannot bring persons into the family relationship. Preaching can inspire some people to *go* to church, but it cannot enable them to *be* the church. We cannot preach people into loving one another.

Pastoral counseling alone is inadequate, if, when a man who comes to us cracking with fear at a crisis in his life and begs us "Teach me to pray!" we give him merely a book on prayer, talk to him about a life of prayer, and assure him that we will pray for him. All these things we may do, but they are not enough. For such a man needs to know that he is undergirded by a brotherhood of persons aware of his need and praying for him. He will learn to pray as a Christian by sharing in the fellowship of a praying people. What do we do with a woman who has been a member of the Christian church for thirty years and says to us, "I want to surrender my life to Christ. I have never fully committed myself to Him. What do I do?" Do we give her a book on commitment, talk to her about it, assure her that she has already been following Christ in some measure? Perhaps, but it is not enough. She needs to be led into a company of pilgrims who are learning to surrender to Christ by walking in mutual surrender to one another.

Where do we put people who are urgent and earnest in their desire to know and serve Christ? How do we deal with them so that they do not embarrass us? Samuel Shoemaker said, "Putting an eager seeker after Christ into the conventional church is like putting a live chicken under a dead hen." We are simply not prepared to handle radical doubt or commitment. Someone becomes fired with real concern but after an evening or two at the Men's Club or the Couples' Club or the Women's Group is overwhelmed with disillusionment.

Here is the major problem. Our conventional structure is not geared to enable people to come into deep personal relationship. Social clubs and groups in the church are at best only a vestibule to the family and may be false substitutes for real belonging together in Christ. The committee structure of churches does not necessitate or even encourage the personal sharing of life which is the heart of the family. In pursuing many useful things, we have neglected the one thing needful. What can we do? How can the conventional church become a family of Christ?

The conventional church will become a family of Christ only for those who find a way of belonging together in a small group of growing, serving Christians. We are not called to walk alone; we are called to share the pilgrimage of a people. We cannot delegate our personal involvement to somebody else. Sending our money will not achieve this involvement; neither will merely sending our children or a husband or wife. Serving on most committees cannot achieve it. Nor will sitting in a pew on Sunday morning by itself. The only way to penetrate the trappings of the life of the modern congregation and to discover the risen Christ is to become personally involved with a few persons in whom He lives and works.

The following account gives an autobiographical picture of a man who has moved *through* the church and finally *into* the church as the family of Christ.

My early religious background was the all-too-common Sunday School mishmash of Old Testament history and customs (the rituals, sacrifices, and symbolism of the early Jews) and a fragmentary picture of Christ as a kindly, gentle shepherd who engaged in an episodic series of miracles. My concept of God was completely vague, as was the relationship between God and Christ. The cross had little real significance. The entire picture was remote, blurred, fictional, with scant relevance to life today.

I joined church as a teenager without preparatory instruction of any kind. Little wonder that it was an impersonal, unimpressive event, not unlike being admitted to a club which had neither membership requirements, nor any strong *raison d'être*. My attendance at church was spasmodic, soon fell away to Easter-Christmas duty visits.

At college I was exposed to no religious influence and can still recall pondering, during reflective moments, the awful possibility that life may be a preamble to nothingness . . . to the terrifying disintegration of self into complete nonexistence, not for a day, or a year, or a century, but for all time and lack of time . . . a cessation of personality, of consciousness, of life . . . forever gone, ended, swallowed up by the blackness of eternal night.

During the years following college I would occasionally go to a nearby church to hear such visiting theological "greats" as Reinhold Niebuhr, Halford Luccock, Paul Tillich, Elmer Homrighausen, and others. But my approach to these exposures was less religious than philosophical, less of the heart than of the mind.

The ineffectiveness of the typical church school noted by this man upsets and confronts us. We are being forced to face the fact that one hour a week is simply insufficient time to give any kind of coherent Christian education. The Supreme Court declarations on prayer and the reading of the Bible in the public schools may help us to discover not only that the public school is not the proper place for religious education but that the church itself is greatly handicapped for the depth work of religious education because of inadequate time and curriculum, and unimaginative approach. How radically to improve the church school is a question for which contemporary churchmen frantically seek answers. Insignificant instruction for membership, the religious "drift" of college years, and the rootlessness of nominal church relationship produce a vast floating "shadow membership" of people on the periphery of the church. Well over half of our church members are, in my judgment, on this periphery.

It was not until I began going regularly to a nearby church and had the continuity of hearing the same minister relate the teachings of Christ to present-day problems in a lucid, logical, often brilliant manner, that the Christian religion began to have relevance. And it was not until this same minister called on us to discuss church membership and referred to me as a sinner . . . a statement that shocked me twice: once when he uttered it, and later when I realized that it *had* shocked me! . . . that I began to realize that Christianity was something which might involve *me*, personally and perhaps intimately.

Joining the First Church thus became a milestone in my spiritual development; the beginning, it might be said, of the "institutional Christianity" phase of my life. As I became acquainted with the members of the fellowship, various organizational activities came my way . . . work on publicity, on the Every-Member-Canvass, ushering, the planning of special programs, and all the busy, busy, busy work which must be done in a large church.

There were real satisfactions in all this activity, not the least of which was a pharisaical feeling of smugness at being so strenuously engaged in the work of the church. I had often heard it said that a person can belong to a church for years—making perfectly splendid contributions to the physical and material life of a parish, necessary and important as these undoubtedly are—without its making a significant difference to his *spiritual* life.

Here is a fair picture of "institutional Christianity," which is not really anyone's fault. It has just grown on us to the place where it now threatens to stultify or snuff out the inner life it was meant to nourish. The insidious danger of "institutional Christianity" is that it is often a false substitute for personal belonging in the family of Christ. It allows us to participate, but not at deep personal levels. It allows us to become organizationally involved but does not threaten to expose or promise to heal our most personal being. It can become a false god protecting us from genuine personal encounter with God and our brothers. Large numbers of our "best people" never get *through* the "work" of the church *into* its spiritual life and mission. They learn how to give time, energy, and money, but not their personal selves. Thus, inevitably, there is a hollowness, unreality, and futility about their church experience.

. . . I was engaged in the business aspect of the church, depending solely upon the ministers to nourish my spiritual needs during the one fleeting Sunday morning hour of worship for the week. I had an intellectual acceptance of the Christian ethic but no deep concern—no sense of personal involvement or commitment. Prayer was on a spasmodic basis and based largely on selfish need or emergency petitioning. I intended to begin systematic reading of the Bible, someday, if this busy, busy pace would ever subside. Perhaps I was waiting for *The Reader's Digest* to publish a condensed version of the New Testament!

Without consistent Bible study, a disciplined life of prayer, and a context for significant sharing of ideas and experience, there can be little sense of personal relationship with God. We

may tip our hats to the Christian ethic but lack the passionate
motivation to seek, discern, and try to do God's will in the
decisions and relationships of everyday life.

A somewhat more laudable activity in which I became engaged,
along with my wife, was the evangelizing call on prospective new
members. This had definite rewards. But I realize now that our
approach was in the best traditions of earnest members of a country
club extending a cordial invitation to some golfers newly arrived in
the neighborhood. By that I mean that we spoke eloquently about our
fine senior minister (the golf pro) and his skill and allure—about
our elaborate physical plant (the club house) and its facilities—about
our fine membership (social rank and status)—but little or nothing
about the opportunity for fellowship in Christ. Although we spoke of
the reverent atmosphere of worship for which our church was noted
and the splendid church music, these clearly were within the frame-
work of the institutional church, not a personal matter of spiritual
enrichment.

I believe my inadequacy was most forcibly revealed to me one
afternoon during a call on a couple who lived in a large apartment
house. The wife, gracious and friendly in manner, clearly was interested in what the church might offer. Her husband, on the other
hand, glowered menacingly at us (when not staring at his TV set),
taking sadistic delight in letting us know that churches were, in his
considered judgment, a damned nuisance, and that he wouldn't be
caught dead in one. In the face of this, we were polite, making feeble
pleas for the value of the church to the lives of people, and what our
church might offer him . . . but all the while lacking the skill, the
fervor, the knowledge of our faith which clearly was needed. How
different, I thought, would be the reaction of a highly trained Com-
munist upon encountering opposition of this sort to *his* "religion"!

The spiritual poverty of the typical church member is un-
veiled in the conversation with the apartment house dweller. Few
of our people are capable of giving forthright, persuasive, and
convincing testimony out of their own personal experience as to
the meaning of life together in the church. Still less are they able
to make a convincing case for the relevance of the church to the
economic and social needs of their immediate community. Having received in the church no "new life in Christ" they cannot

give this life to the world. They are unequipped to be soldiers or ambassadors of Christ.

I observed that most congregations looked to their ministers to provide the spiritual life of the church, depending upon them, in a sense, to predigest the teachings of Christ and spoonfeed the more palatable portions to the passive pew-sitter along with a generous dosage of paregoric to deaden any feeling of sin or guilt.

The more successful a minister became in making of Christianity a comforting and soothing gospel, the greater his popularity and reputation among those who worshiped—not God—but "our minister," and the more attention he attracted from other congregations which were seeking an outstanding pulpit man for *their* church. Thus was perpetuated the mad competitive scramble from coast to coast by churches whose memberships were built up, or deteriorated, depending upon how successful or unsuccessful they were in attracting personalities who could "pack them in." I began to sense that true spiritual strength could be attained only if the *members* of a church truly became the *church*—the body of Christ—with their pastor looked to chiefly for instruction, for guidance, for inspiration, and for co-ordination of their efforts.

Gradually came a realization that certain imperatives, certain prerequisites of true Christian discipleship simply were not a part of my life. I lacked grounding in Christian beliefs; I adhered to no discipline of prayer or study; I had no training for, or experience of, Christian witness, and felt no sense of personal mission. I became aware of my need to dig deeper into the faith.

Disillusionment with the "successful" church and minister is widespread among sensitive laymen and clergy. There is a growing realization of our spiritual shallowness and a desire to begin doing something about it. When we become afflicted with the gnawing hunger of spiritual emptiness, we are ready and willing to enter upon serious discipleship. We will make the sacrifices of time and priority which are required. We will relinquish our precious privacy in the acknowledgment that we cannot find that for which we hunger alone. We are ready for a corporate pilgrimage.

A significant step forward was the formation of a *koinonia* group of which my wife and I became members. Consisting of seventeen men and women of dissimilar backgrounds and temperament, who met bi-weekly for prayer, worship, study, and Christian sharing, this group took on a new and interesting dimension. There was participation in spoken prayer . . . for me, an unaccustomed practice. There were periods of silence and contemplation, all too infrequent in modern living. There was programmed study of Scripture and related commentaries, with opportunity to raise questions and take part in the search for answers. There was the intersharing of experiences, reactions, doubts, fears, hopes, and convictions, from which emerged a growing realization that *all* in the group were searching, exploring, struggling. Although we represented a diversity of cultural backgrounds, vocations, educational training, temperaments, and beliefs, we slowly but steadily began forging bonds of sympathy, understanding, and concern which linked us in a fellowship in Christ . . . a little Christian family, in a sense . . . which led to the bearing of one another's burdens, the offering of prayers for one another, the development of a genuine spirit of *koinonia*.[4]

Out of this experience have come two insights: first, the realization that we are privileged to have a depth relationship with these folk, seldom duplicated even in friendships of many years' standing; secondly, that we have acquired an appreciation for the great worth of people of different racial and cultural backgrounds, so that in place of impersonal generalizations we now have personal affection and esteem for particular persons we have come to know and cherish.

A *koinonia* group, or some similar prayer, study, or discussion group, is often the first exposure to a close personal relationship even faintly resembling that described in the New Testament. If the church is to be the school of discipleship where we learn to love one another as Christ has loved us, it can happen only by means of some small-group involvement. If personhood blossoms in community, then the church must find ways of becoming a genuine family in which persons discover one another as brothers and sisters. In local churches of several hundred members or more, there seems to be no workable alternative to the small-group approach, in seeking to provide a context for developing deep personal friendship.

Another significant and richly rewarding experience of growth was our Men's Retreat. This was my first retreat, and I looked forward to it with mingled feelings of optimism, curiosity, and a certain vagueness as to the outcome. As we began to associate together, the seventeen of us, under the disciplines laid down by our leaders, I could sense the birth of a comradeship which differed from anything I had ever experienced before. Our periods of silence were refreshing and invigorating, not merely for the absence of ringing phones, blaring TV and radio, incessant chatter, and all the Babel which so often assails our tortured ears, but for the sense of communion which developed in performing simple tasks with others, without conversing or verbalizing our thoughts, yet communicating in a brotherly way through nods, smiles, or simple gestures. The opportunities for contemplation, for quiet reading, for dining together in silence, except for inspirational ideas shared with us by a designated reader, for the exchange of experiences and observations during the discussion periods, for worship and prayer together in simplicity and spontaniety—all these created a community among us, a sense of brotherhood, an awareness of our common sonship. And gradually we realized that the outer veneers, the layers of "self-preserving" sophistication with which we surround ourselves, were being cast off, discarded, freeing us to respond to each other without barriers, without reserve, without "role-playing."

But the high point and climax was the sharing of Communion together in the Lodge on the mountaintop. This, truly, was a "mountaintop" experience. As each man offered publicly his prayer of confession —a prayer which was individual and personal to the petitioner—all of us realized full well that the next man's prayer actually was *our* prayer too . . . that we *all* were bearing the sins of the entire group and thus stood in need of forgiveness and grace. And as each man partook of the bread and the wine, with all others around the table praying silently for him, we became overwhelmingly conscious of the presence of the Holy Spirit as though in this moment, with all earthly ties and concerns severed and time seeming to stand still, we were suddenly in the very presence of Christ, exposed to His searching gaze, without a semblance of pretense or pride or guile.

It was interesting and perhaps significant that after this two-day retreat, I felt more refreshed and renewed than after many two- or three-week vacations. Also, I returned with an overpowering feeling of elation, as though this was something I coveted for everyone I knew and loved, something I desired to share with others.

A retreat can be a time of awakening, remarkable in power and possibility for the participant. Personal and corporate breakthroughs occur which simply would not have taken place in the normal course of events. Telescoping into two days the hours of sharing which might otherwise have taken many weeks drives the personal relationships deep. The quiet hours of reflection and personal research provide the climate for fresh surges of creativity and hope. New perspectives and directions rise up. It is as though one had discovered an oasis in the spiritual desert and began to drink deeply of its restorative waters. A new and joyous brotherhood emerges.

Note especially the profound meaning of Holy Communion on this retreat. Communion is not intended to create fellowship in Christ but to embody it, to represent it, to express it. When Communion is shared by people who are already bound together as members of the family of Christ, it is indeed the great sacrament of His presence. Dietrich Bonhoeffer writes,

The day of the Lord's Supper is an occasion of joy for the Christian community. Reconciled in their hearts with God and the brethren, the congregation receives the gift of the body and blood of Jesus Christ, and, receiving that, it receives forgiveness, new life, and salvation. It is given new fellowship with God and men. The fellowship of the Lord's Supper is the superlative fulfillment of Christian fellowship. As the members of the congregation are united in body and blood at the table of the Lord so will they be together in eternity. Here the community has reached its goal. Here joy in Christ and His community is complete. The life of Christians together under the Word has reached its perfection in the sacrament.[5]

How pale our typical Sunday Communion seems in contrast to all that is described above!

Real communion (*koinonia*) with the Lord and with one another releases the gifts of ministry and transforms the church into a ministering community.

I found myself involved as a lay minister in training new people for membership in the church. *Christian Faith and Life* classes proved to be a most exciting and satisfying form of ministry. The contacts, taking place on six evenings at weekly intervals, provided sufficient continuity and duration to "minister" to people in a meaningful way.

With the topic of the evening expounded by the minister during his talk to the entire group, the lay people were able to "pick up" the theme and launch into conversation with those comprising the various discussion groups into which the "students" were divided. It was most interesting to see how this group of strangers, at first somewhat reluctant to participate in any extended discussion, gradually began to feel a part of a congenial assembly of fellowseekers as the evenings progressed. Some who refrained almost determinedly from taking part during the first sessions soon were unburdening themselves privately (and sometimes publicly) of problems, anxieties, apprehensions, which had muted their desire to be more outgoing. It was a great satisfaction to see the tremendous change which could take place in these folk in just a few weeks; strangers becoming friends; a group of individuals welding into a more or less cohesive fellowship; a genuine concern developing on the part of each lay leader for his "flock," and on the part of the flock for the leaders as well as for other members of the group.

In fact, this epitomizes one of the insights which thus far has impressed me as I seek to find what it means to be a Christian: namely, that to work at being a Christian, really to get involved with other people in the role of minister or servant, converts us from the passive role of merely studying to the added active role of doing and thus understanding Christ "from the inside."

The corollary to this is the strengthening of faith which results, because we begin to see the miracle of lives changed and transformed through fellowship in Him. It is as though we had long hoped we were justified in believing in the existence of electricity, but with the lighting up of a thousand radiant bulbs we suddenly realized that "here it is, at work, glowing and vital, demonstrated before our eyes," even though we still are incapable of defining, blueprinting, or analyzing into its constituent parts the electricity of the Holy Spirit.

Ministry is the fruit of belonging to Christ and learning His love. As the writer received the gift of Christ's love in the *koinonia* group and retreat experiences, he became aware of his mission to share this gift with others, to take up his ministry in church and world.

So here I am . . . a little bit along a road of indeterminate length, and leading me I know not where. Of one thing I am certain: the journey will be a long one and, I suspect, I shall always be in the beginning stages. In fact, I sometimes ask myself: "Are you making significant progress?" And the honest answer is not too comforting. I still feel so much on the surface with a lack of true depth, as though the roots might still be in shallow soil with insufficient nourishment to withstand a real drought.

I do feel, with Dietrich Bonhoeffer, the need for alternate periods of withdrawal and of outgoing participation, of study and renewal, and of ministry and sharing. How wise he was when he observed that a man incapable of one is unworthy for the other! The great pitfalls, I feel, are those of turning to withdrawal as a means of escape, of responding to the ego, instead of to the Holy Spirit, and of falling into the easy sin of self-righteousness. These, and the ever-present danger of worshiping false gods, will give me a busy time, I suspect, in striving to keep on compass.

Perhaps this man's testimony will encourage others to make their own pilgrimage from the periphery of the church, or from "institutional Christianity," into the family of Christ and participation in the ministering community. This is the hope for contemporary Christendom: that the conventional church may begin to take the shape of the family of Christ.

Where there is a family of Christ there is the possibility of the army of the Lord.

Chapter 3

The Army of the Lord

And his gifts were that some should be apostles, some
prophets, some evangelists, some pastors and teachers, for
the equipment of the saints, for the work of ministry. . . .
Ephesians 4:11-12

The church's mission is not primarily to bring the world into the church but to *be* the church in the world. We are a world-oriented people. Our task is to participate in God's mission there—the God who so loved the world He gave His son, who sent the Son not to condemn but to save the world, who was in Christ reconciling the world to Himself. Jesus told the disciples that they were the salt of the *earth*, the light of the *world*, the leaven of the *lump*, sheep in the midst of *wolves*. We are sent-people, apostles, missionaries. The world is the field of our mission.

This has meant for me something of a reversal, a turning inside out. Hendrik Kraemer has written that ". . . every Christian needs two conversions: first to Christ and then to the world. . . ."[1] I have been going through my conversion to the world in recent years. I have come to see that our fellowship in the Lord becomes a sanctified dead end unless it enables us to bear fruit for God in the world. The church focused on the growth of

its internal life together is the family of Christ. The church preparing for its mission in the world is the army of the Lord. In
Chapters 4 and 5 we shall consider the shape of our mission in
the world. In this chapter we shall consider the church's mobilization for this mission.

It seems ridiculous to think of the modern church as an army.
The prosperous suburban church may be enjoying the spoils of
a Pyrrhic victory in its satellite culture. The inner-city church
may be desperately fighting a rearguard action. The urban
church may be fending off foes without and foes within; and yet
it would hardly appear to the outsider that the hymn writer was
right when he wrote, "Like a mighty army moves the church of
God."[2] In terms of the perspective of history, perhaps; but in
terms of St. John's-by-the-gas-station, probably not.

Yet the image of the army is pertinent and useful.[3] We are
reminded that the church is engaged in battle "against the
spiritual hosts of wickedness" (Eph. 6:12). There is an urgency
about our existence as Christians. The time for battle is always
now. Therefore, the church is always engaged in the complex
process of mobilization. The church is always trying to marshal
its forces and deploy them strategically in the battle for the
minds and spirits of men. The church is constantly in need of appraising its strategy and redefining its mission in the light of new
information about "the enemy."

One of the striking facts described in Barbara Tuchman's *The
Guns of August*[4] is the stupidity of the French generals, who
were so intent on their own fixed plan of attack that they literally
could not hear and believe reports from their own scouts about
the movements of German troops, reports which should have
caused them to alter radically their own strategy. They were
blind to the truth that might have saved them. Those of us who
are staff sergeants in the army of the Lord like to think that it is
the generals of the church who make all the blunders, who are
blind to the truth we, their scouts, faithfully report. And it is a
fact that generals make mistakes just as surely as do staff sergeants.

However, the whole church at every level of its leadership and in every location of its life is in danger of fiercely fighting battles against enemies that have silently slipped away to take us by surprise elsewhere. We must scout out our contemporary world by listening to the poets, artists, statesmen, and plain people who are its spokesmen. We must locate the most dangerous enemies and devise our strategy for effective militant action on today's battlefields.

The parish church is local headquarters for the army of the Lord in its community. It is the base of operations for the soldiers of Christ in that place. It is their drill hall, their strategy clinic, their hospital for the wounded and beaten, their center for regrouping and shaping new plans of defense and attack. Above all, it is the focal point where Christians are equipped for mission. Just as the logistics and organizational superstructure of an army are solely the means of preparing it for its varied missions, so the institutional paraphernalia of the local congregation are solely the means of preparing Christ's soldiers for their mission. Structures in the local church that are peripheral or irrelevant to this preparation must be reshaped where possible and sloughed off where necessary.

There are three essential marks of the reshaping of the local church into the army of the Lord. First, *there is a new kind of recruitment.* In more traditional terms, there is a new concept of discipleship and a new method of invitation to discipleship. Dietrich Bonhoeffer has described the conventional concept of discipleship in terms of what he calls "cheap grace": "Cheap grace is the preaching of forgiveness without requiring repentance, baptism without Church discipline, Communion without confession, absolution without contrition. Cheap grace is grace without discipleship, grace without the Cross, grace without Jesus Christ, living and incarnate."[5]

It is easy to document this cheap grace. We are all guilty of persuading someone to join the church of Christ before he is ready for meaningful commitment to Christian discipleship. A bulletin of a church came to my desk some time ago, across the top of which were three phrases—the message of that church to its visitors: "air-conditioned, comfortably seated, beautifully furnished." (Recently this unholy Trinity was removed.) I noted that early in the service there was an invitation for anyone who wished to come forward and, by assenting to a few words, become a member of the church—that is to say, commit himself to being a soldier of Christ in the army of the Lord.

Where is the cross in our invitation to discipleship? It has disappeared, and in its place is a genial handshake. We sweep in the sheep and proudly note them in our registers of salvation-by-works at the next Annual Conference. What a sharp contrast between this procedure and the manner in which Jesus invited persons to become His disciples. He was always cautioning them against too early, too quick, too superficial discipleship. "If any man would come after me, let him deny himself and take up his cross and follow me" (Mark 8:34); "if any one . . . does not hate his own father and mother and wife and children and brothers and sisters, yes, and even his own life, he cannot be my disciple" (Luke 14:26); "For whoever would save his life will lose it" (Mark 8:35).

According to the Gospel of John, many disciples drew back after Jesus' hard sayings about discipleship (6:66). Jesus lost some very good people, including the rich young ruler (Mark 10:17-31). Halford Luccock used to say that we modern churchmen would have taken that rich young ruler and made him Chairman of the Finance Commission, saying to ourselves, "He'll grow, he'll grow."

The time has come to recover the integrity of membership in the Christian church. We must present the gospel in its full reality in terms of what Bonhoeffer calls "costly grace."

Costly grace is the treasure hidden in the field; for the sake of it a man will gladly go and sell all that he has. It is the pearl of great price to buy which the merchant will sell all his goods. . . . it is the call of Jesus Christ at which the disciple leaves his nets and follows Him. . . .

Such grace is *costly* because it calls us to follow, and it is *grace* because it calls us to follow *Jesus Christ*. It is costly because it costs a man his life and it is grace because it gives a man the only true life.[6]

How can we invite people into this kind of discipleship? It is clear that we cannot do so effectively any longer by sending laymen to call on them in their homes and invite them then and there to "make a decision for Christ." Most modern men are not able to "hear" the gospel of costly grace that clearly and quickly. They readily, and often rightly, suspect the church of institutional hucksterism when we approach them with handy commitment cards. Increasing numbers of people living in metropolitan areas are just plain bored with church, or disillusioned by what they know of it. They will not be won to Christ by a friendly call alone.

Nor can we responsibly summon people to costly discipleship by a cordial pastoral invitation in the context of worship. William Lazareth writes,

People have a right to know that when we invite them to become fellow disciples we are not merely offering them an emotional jag or intellectual exercise, or a sure key to happiness and success. We are asking them, rather, to permit God to transform them and their entire existence from self-centeredness to God-centeredness, from self-worship to the worship of a crucified and risen Lord.[7]

This call to commitment cannot be given by a few words of invitation or in an hour's informal chat in the minister's home the night before new members are to be received. A meaningful context for such invitation to discipleship must be found.

Such a context is provided by a series of meetings to which persons interested in membership may be invited. In the church I currently serve, these meetings are titled "Christian Faith and Life Class." At each meeting a lecture is given by the minister on a major doctrine of Christian faith. People then are divided into small groups where discussion of the lecture is led by laymen.[8]

The context of the small group and the encounter with concerned Christian laymen allows the Word literally to become flesh in the developing relationships. Strangers find themselves welcomed into a fellowship whose reality surprises and arrests them. Curiosity deepens into the hope that perhaps here are people who know something firsthand of the living God. It may be a new insight gained from a lecture or one of the books offered for loan or purchase, or from a biblical verse in the weekly assignment. It may be the comment of someone in the discussion group. It may be a spark of excitement at the discovery that the church is involved significantly in serving its community. It may be the genuine friendship of a lay leader whose telephone call or note or personal visit underlines the truth that one is honestly cared for by these people. By one means or another the stranger begins to hear the gospel of costly grace in a new key, and to understand that Christian faith and life may be far more demanding and fulfilling than he had realized. At the end of such a course we can responsibly invite people to commit themselves to Christian discipleship, content that the Lord shall confirm whom He will.

A word of caution. We are seeking to embody the gospel and to invite persons to share the life of the risen Christ with us. We can only share what we are. The reality or superficiality of our fellowship in Christ will be exposed in the meetings, where we become visible and vulnerable. This means that the preparation of leaders, lay and ministerial, is of crucial importance. Knowledge of the subjects to be discussed and skill in the techniques of effective group discussion are indispensable. Several preparatory sessions to enable the leaders to grow in such knowledge and skill are necessary. Equally necessary is the spiritual preparation of the leaders prior to each meeting. The minister and lay leaders in our church meet one hour before the class begins for our own worship and consecration to the ministry of that particular evening. During that hour we worship through Scripture, silence, and the sharing of thoughts and experience pertinent to the evening's discussion theme. We pray for one another that we may be empowered to conduct our evening ministries in the spirit. We pray that the people coming to the meetings will have their minds opened to the gospel, and that we may be sensitive to their needs and responsive to their concerns. We offer ourselves in the manner of Jesus: "And for their sake I consecrate myself, that they also may be consecrated in truth" (John 17:19).

If the context for the invitation to discipleship is a "Christian Faith and Life" class of this kind, in our initial contacts with new people we will invite them to participate in the life and work of the church. We can urge them, without apology or hypocrisy, to take part in a study group or a service project, or to worship with us. We can invite them into whatever area of the church's life seems most immediately relevant to them. At this point the conventional social groups of the church may have a valid function. Such a group is the least threatening kind of structure into which a stranger may go. If the committed church members of these groups regard themselves and their group as a vehicle for drawing strangers more deeply into the church, significant evangelism can be carried on in the social setting. A social group *can* be a vestibule into the heart of the church's life and mission. Our hope is that, wherever the new person touches the perimeter of the church's fellowship, he will be moved and grasped by what he sees and hears. When the time is right, and he begins to ask serious questions, he is invited to come to the meetings described above, and to consider committing himself to Christian discipleship.

Such a strategy provides a crucial opportunity to reshape the church of today and tomorrow. In our mobile society we are constantly receiving as well as losing members. Over a period of several years a church in a metropolitan area may well experience a 50 per cent turnover of membership. A strong, focused membership-training mission can be the agent of transformation of the local congregation, *if* what happens after reception into membership is not "assimilation" but equipment for the tasks of congregational and personal mission. And here is the difficulty: we win people to some real measure of Christian discipleship, and then their zeal wanes in the confusion of activities in the conventional congregation, whose program often looks more like that of a circus than of an army. The first mark of the reshaping of a church as the army of the Lord is a new kind of recruitment.

Second, *there is a new kind of equipment*. The purpose of our life together as Christians is to prepare us for effective Christian living in the world. It is the task of the church to equip its people for congregational and personal mission. There are limits to the mission fields for which the local church should prepare its members. Each congregation needs to define the missionary areas of its primary competence and responsibility and to perceive its peculiar vocation in the unfolding purpose of God. It is then free to rejoice in the specialized ministries, both traditional and experimental, provided for in mission fields outside its own purview.

At the same time, the local church should rightly seek to expose its people to the whole of life in its cultural setting. In appropriate ways every church must seek to enable its members to be whole persons in the variety of ministries they perform in daily life and work. The particularity of the mission fields responsibly chosen by a local church will depend upon such factors as its size, location, congregational make-up, etc. *Every local church needs to define its own mission fields and appraise its congregational program in terms of its effectiveness or irrelevance to the task of equipping its people for mission.*

Let us examine three fields of mission which, in some fashion and to some degree, every local church will acknowledge as its responsibility.

1. *Family*. The mission field most readily understood and accepted by the local church is the family life of its members and those who live near them. Because it is a familiar focus of mission, let us not underrate its importance or think that we have effec-

tively solved all the problems of Christian family living. The real question is, How can a family of Christians become a family of Christ? How can members of a family belong to one another in Christ, learn to love one another in Christ's love, and release the gifts of mutual ministry? How can the church begin to take shape in the home?

Let me sketch some specific ways in which we can equip our people for Christian marriage and Christian nurture.

a. *Christian marriage*. A *koinonia* group can be a valuable means of equipping a husband or a wife for creative marriage. It may be wise for one partner to participate in such a group by himself, finding in fellowship with others the forgiveness and freedom not yet discovered with the married partner. Especially if he has minor emotional problems he may be better able to find healing in the unconscious therapy of a group without the presence of the married partner. (Such an experience is related in Chapter 6.) On the other hand, couples in the group have the advantage of discovering and sharing a new dimension of relationship together. Problems are unearthed or brought into discussion which have existed but not been recognized or acknowledged. Husband and wife find themselves talking over matters of faith and life which they had previously found neither occasion nor time to discuss. The group provokes the possibility of more honest and sensitive communication, opening doors of acceptance and understanding.

Special seminars for married couples can be held to discuss such books as *The Creative Years* and *Herein Is Love* by Reuel Howe. In one such seminar a couple realized with a shock that instead of sharing their lives each had been going off in his own direction. They missed the last two meetings of the seminar because they decided to take a two-week vacation to renew their marriage! Retreats for married couples provide another means of arraying them for, and healing them in, Christian marriage.

The necessity for thorough premarital counseling by the minister is increasingly clear. For many years I was content to have an hour's session with young couples prior to their wedding. Some time ago a fellow minister showed me how inadequate that preparation was and introduced me to a more complete and significant premarital counseling procedure. (See the outline of five counseling sessions in Appendix 3.)

In addition to adequate counseling, we need to find ways of celebrating the *Christian* significance of approaching marriage. Recently a group of women in a local church held a special kind of shower for a young woman of the church about to be married. They gave her gifts not only material but spiritual. One woman spoke, for all, of the pain and joy of being a Christian wife and mother. She concluded, "We want you to know that we are your friends and partners. We want you to feel free to ask help of any of us. With you we join now in renewing our own vows of marriage and bind ourselves to encourage and strengthen you in the sacred duties of wife and mother." The shower was ended with prayer. The church surrounded this young woman with the love of Christ and celebrated her entrance upon Christian marriage.

b. *Christian nurture.* The occasion of a child's baptism is a rare chance to reach parents at a new depth. Hearts are open; and if the appropriate kind of confrontation occurs, real awakenings can take place and new directions can be taken. For several years we have asked parents whose children are soon to be baptized to come together for an instruction meeting. At the meeting the minister points out that in the vow of the baptism ceremony parents make an unconditional commitment to do all they can by "precept and example" to lead their children to know and serve God. A lay couple of the church then emphasizes the fact that parents bear the chief responsibility for the Christian education of their children, and that they themselves must grow in their faith if they are to be able to share it effectively with their children. Such lay witness is often provocative and moving. Again and again parents have said that it was after this prebaptismal meeting that they decided to become involved in a study group or in one of the missions of the church. The congregational priesthood implicit in the lay leadership of the meeting is made explicit in the vow spoken by all church members at the conclusion of the sacrament of baptism celebrated, as it ought to be, during the

Sunday worship of the family of Christ. The vow reads, "We rejoice to receive these children into the family of Christ in this place. We pledge ourselves as their friends, counselors, and fellow pilgrims on the Christian way, to guide them by our precept and example that they and we may grow in the knowledge and love of God according to the measure of the stature of the fullness of Christ. Amen."

Many church educators and parents are agreed that our present Christian education of children and young people is inadequate. It is much less clear how the conventional Sunday school can be reshaped, or some other means found to equip our young people for effective Christian living. Two directions are being taken that may be mentioned here. First, some churches are inaugurating classes in which both parents and children must enroll. The parents are in class at the same time as their children, being taught how to teach their own children in the home. The purpose is to equip parents for the task of Christian education and worship in the home. Second, some churches are moving toward a much more academic training for junior and senior high young people. Whether in the traditional Sunday morning class or on Saturday or some other day, pamphlets and booklets are being discarded in favor of books. Assignments are made, themes are written, and examinations are held. A serious attempt is made to present the faith in its objective doctrinal and ethical outline to young people before they go to college. Today it is necessary to enable youth to understand the Bible and Christian theology in terms commensurate with modern science and psychology. In many churches the confirmation class is held over the period of a year or longer, and appropriate books on doctrine, church history, and ethics are used rather than the customary booklets. Every local church might well consider making similar ventures in its own task of educating young people for Christian living.

2. *Work*. The second mission field for which the local church is responsible, if not so clearly competent, is daily work and the

economic structures of society. There is perhaps no area of modern life for which the church is less effectively instructing its people. At a retreat on Christian Faith and Occupation some years ago, the confusion of "good church members" as to the relation of their faith to daily work was appalling. Evident in some men was a deep sense of guilt in the belief that one really *couldn't* be a Christian in the workaday world and still move ahead profitably. What does it mean to turn the other cheek to one's competitor? How does one "love" his neighbor in the form of buyer, seller, employee, employer, boss, subordinate? Most men thought of the relevance of faith to work in terms of personal relationships, not in terms of decision making or of appraising corporate policy and structure. Other men declared too painlessly and breezily that they operated their businesses by the Sermon on the Mount or lived at work according to the Golden Rule.

Ministers are often unable to be of help to businessmen seeking to be Christian in daily work because of their ignorance of the world of business, industry, unions, and management. Ministers have so often held forth from the pulpit about complex industrial issues, giving simplistic or moralistic prescriptions for illnesses they do not begin to understand, that they have virtually forfeited the right to be heard. Perhaps this is good, too, in that it teaches us that it is now time for ministers to listen rather than to be heard. They might begin by reading *Ethics and Business* by William Spurrier.[9]

The church must provide for serious and open communication between clergy and businessmen, and the local church can be the place for it. Vocational study groups bring together men and women in the same profession to consider their particular field and its peculiar ethical problems in the light of Christian faith. Other study groups can focus on broader aspects of the changing industrial economy: unemployment, automation, collective bargaining, and the role of government.

The job situation can be the place for communication between concerned laymen with or without a minister present. Meeting at lunch, or before or after hours, participants discuss issues that arise out of their own work structures, seeking to interpret these issues in terms of Christian faith. Where non-Christians are present, the traditional religious language—words like "sin," "grace," "salvation"—will not be used, and Christ or God will seldom be referred to. Operating from the stance of his own faith, the Christian will seek to interpret the meaning and value he perceives in specific issues in terminology current and acceptable to all concerned. It remains for some laymen, as well as theologians and sociologists, to carve out a Christian posture and vocabulary shaped by work structures and relevant to them.[10]

3. *Community.* The third mission field in which the local congregation has special competence and responsibility is its own neighborhood and the wider metropolitan area. It is primarily, or at least initially, in "Jerusalem" (Acts 1:8) that we are called to be witnesses. It is the task of the local church to discipline its people for effective congregational and personal mission in the social, political, and cultural structures of society.

Once again, we should begin by becoming informed about the real nature of the community, its power structure, its financial resources, its racial and ethnic groupings, its problems and human needs. The church must listen before it acts or speaks.

One urban church invited twelve of the leaders in its neighborhood to come to a meeting in the church building and tell the church what the community needs were. Among the needs revealed were a day-care nursery for working mothers, an after-school-hours recreation program for youth, a vocational training program for youth unskilled for other than a laboring job, and a tutoring program for high school youth about to drop out of school. That church undertook a tutoring program as its first serious attempt to serve the people living in the church's immediate neighborhood. Within three months, fifteen church members were tutoring over forty students two nights a week in church classrooms. The courses covered the range of a typical high school curriculum. Personal relationships of real significance developed between tutors and pupils, including, in many cases, the pupil's entire family. A few persons came into the life of the church through such relationships, although this was not the purpose or intent of the tutoring program itself. Involvement in the tutoring program uncovered and made possible other ways of serving the neighborhood. The beginning of such service was the church's willingness to listen to, and learn from, its community.

The local church should equip its people to deal creatively with the broad range of human problems, from urban renewal and local politics to mental health and international relations. It is clear that one local church by itself does not possess all the resources for leadership that are necessary for this kind of task. Co-operative ventures will be required, bringing together persons from many different churches who share a common interest in a particular community or national problem.

The church, reshaped as the army of the Lord, will recruit and equip its people for imaginative and dramatic appearance in the world. Much of the world thinks it knows what the church is like and has dismissed it as irrelevant to the currents of modern history and, worse yet, irredeemably dull! We must find new ways of being the church in the world so as to surprise the world. This means that we must break out of our Gothic, Georgian, or con-crete-block walls to carry new and arresting shapes out where people live, work, and play.

Third, *there is a new kind of deployment.* Once we have gathered and trained our forces, how can we most expeditiously send them to, and place them in, "enemy territory"? What is our strategy of deployment? What are the new shapes of mission? The fact that such questions are being raised in seminaries and churches today is highly significant. It means that we are indeed in a time of reformation—reformation of church structures (ecclesiology) and reformation of the church's understanding of itself and the world (theology). It is the time predicted by F. D. Maurice, a British theologian of the nineteenth century, when he said, "I cannot but think that the reformation in our day, which I expect to be more deep and searching than that of the sixteenth century, will turn upon the Spirit's presence and life, as that did upon the justification by the Son."[11] It is the Holy Spirit who creates and renews the church of Jesus Christ, pouring out the wine of new life and making plain the inadequacy of the old wineskins.

Such a time is inevitably and necessarily a time for experimentation. In trial and error the church must grope its way into the shadowed highways and byways of the world. We do not discover the new shapes of mission by imposing our clever ideas on the world. God reveals the new shapes to us as we become painfully and humbly involved in the world and exposed to its skeptical indifference or ridicule or hostility. We must expect a high degree of failure as we search and re-search for the new kinds of deployment. I was struck by a full-page advertisement in *The New York Times* in which the eye-catching phrase leaped out, "Odds are 9 to 1 it fails."[12] The advertisement was explaining the odds for failure or success of new products on the market, and the necessity for companies to be constantly turning out experimental products. Occasionally, it said, a product appears that opens up a vast new market, making all the failures small in contrast with its success.

So the church and its leadership must have the courage and hope to allow experimentation within the conventional structures, experimentation which may seem at times like deviation. The maverick should be counseled and understood, not crudely disciplined. We never know—we who follow in the train of Amos, John the Baptist, Jesus, Paul, Luther, Wesley, William Booth, and a host of other rebels and nonconformists—when another prophet, major or minor, may be concealed within the most unlikely man with a vision or a dream. In fact, we are told that in a time of reformation "young men shall see visions, and . . . old men shall dream dreams" (Acts 2:17). And, brethren, we are low enough on prophets so that we cannot afford to lose or discourage a single one!

May the leadership of the church have the faith to experiment and the courage to cut losses when it is necessary to do so. We shall discover the new shapes of mission only by trying and failing and trying again. From such trials here and there across the country, fragments of answers are beginning to appear for our questions about the new kind of deployment. Let me mention briefly a few that may be provocative for you and your church.

1. *Open-door policy*. Simple and obvious as it may sound, a church begins the new deployment by making its facilities available for the world to use. An urban church, blessed with a beautiful chapel with an entrance on the street, had closed its chapel door for several years in fear of the deteriorating neighborhood around it. After considerable discussion and heart searching, the officials of the church opened the chapel on a twenty-four-hour-a-day basis. A guard was stationed in a hall adjoining the chapel from the hours of 10:00 P.M. to 4:00 A.M. both for the protection of the chapel and in order to determine the extent of its use during night hours. It was discovered that more than two hundred people a month came into the chapel between those hours! Eventually the guard was replaced by an excellent alarm system. That church opened its doors to its neighborhood as if to say, "We are not afraid of you any longer; we want to know you and serve you." What facilities in your church could be made available, or more accessible, to your community?

2. *Joint visitation of newcomers*. Two Methodist churches in the city, one predominantly Negro and the other predominantly white, joined their Commissions on Christian Social Concerns to concentrate together on a depressed area near both churches. After several months of conversation, a group of twenty men, ten from each church, was formed to make personal calls on families moving into an urban redevelopment housing project built in the depressed area. Each calling unit included one man from each church. The purpose of the joint visitation was to welcome new-

comers to the community and extend to them in this fashion an invitation to both churches. With what other churches in your community could your church co-operate in such an interracial, interchurch, or interdenominational effort?

3. *Shapes of mission in secular structures.* A suburban church started a Bible study group in an apartment building for elderly people in the central part of their city. The purpose of the group was to go where there was human need, providing discussion and fellowship for those who wanted it. The possibility of such groups, formed in homes for the aged, nursing homes, children's homes, etc., is without limit. Elton Trueblood has described the same sort of penetration into prisons.[13] University communities provide similar opportunities for a local church, or laymen from several local churches, to take missionary shape in some form of action or fellowship on the campus.

4. *Focus on specific sectors of culture.* An arts festival was held in the First Methodist Church of Germantown in the fall of 1962.[14] The purpose was to demonstrate and dramatize the church's concern for art and the artist. The festival began on Friday night with a drama in the church sanctuary by a professional New York Company. On Saturday there were workshops in such allied fields of interest as "Religion in Modern Poetry," "Rhythmic Movement," "Audio-Visual Aids and the Arts," "Theology and Art," etc. The church gymnasium was transformed into an art gallery that exhibited the finest religious art of all faiths obtainable from local artists, and gallery talks were given by an art critic. The festival was climaxed Sunday afternoon with a performance of *The Peaceable Kingdom* sung by five church choirs and conducted by the composer Randall Thompson. Hundreds of persons outside the church participated in some aspect of the festival, and discovered in a fresh way the concern of the church for art.

A local church or a group of local churches can focus the

church's concern on modern science, work and economic structures, government and political structures, and the field of education. The form of such focus may be a festival weekend, a weekend conference, or a series of speakers and workshops over several
weeks, followed by study groups of awakened and interested persons in the churches of the community. Could your church or the
churches of your community manage something of this kind?

5. _New structures._ The Coffee House of the Church of the
Saviour in Washington, D.C., is perhaps the most famous example
of the church's appearance in a new shape in the world.[15] Other
coffee houses inspired by it are cropping up across the country.
A bookstore in Burlington, Vermont, called "The Loft" was
started and is operated by a church. The purpose of the store is
to serve people in this particular way, opening up the possibility
of relationship and dialogue with many who would never find
their way through the door of the conventional church on Sunday morning. There is a small room in a business and professional
building in the town of Wilton, Connecticut, with the name
"Ecumenical Centre."[16] The result of conversations among laymen and clergy from several churches, the Centre is an attempt
to let the church take shape in the midst of the work structures
of society. Its current focus is on vocational study groups.

Whatever the kind of deployment, the church will in every
case take the form of a _servant people_, meeting a genuine human
need without ulterior motive. In the context of this servanthood,
the church will appear appropriately as the witnessing community. The next two chapters will illustrate by concrete examples how mission groups can go forth from the army of the
Lord to take the shape of Christ in the world.

Chapter 4

The Servant People

> "... for I was hungry and you gave me food, I
> was thirsty and you gave me drink, I was a stranger
> and you welcomed me, I was naked and you clothed
> me, I was sick and you visited me, I was in prison and
> you came to me.... Truly, I say to you, as you did
> it to one of the least of these my brethren, you did
> it to me."
>
> *Matthew 25: 35-36, 40*

An army is equipped and disciplined to ready itself for a
specific mission. The army of the Lord has received its assignment
from Christ: to minister in the world and to the world after the
pattern He set—in the form of a servant. What it means for the
church to be a servant people will vary with the setting, the capacity, the alertness of each congregation. But perhaps the main
features of our common mission can be traced in the story of one
response to one challenge in a representative church situation.

The inner-city section of Cleveland has existed in its present
state for a long time. Even "the best location in the nation,"
according to the slogan of a local utility company, has its slums.
There the Negroes and the poor whites from West Virginia or
Pennsylvania come to work and live. They may be joined by
Puerto Ricans, as on the West Side of Cleveland. They are the

poor, the weak, the uneducated, the sick, the unemployed—and some of them the unemployable—people of our culture.

Several years ago, recognizing the need for a specialized ministry to the people of this area, the Inner City Parish was organized. A group ministry involving ministers and their families came into being. These families lived right in the middle of the slum areas and identified themselves with the people. Storefronts and other similar structures were used to bring the church into that world. People who would never walk into a Gothic stone cathedral might look through the window of a storefront. Many urban and suburban churches of main-line Protestant denominations supported this work from the beginning, chiefly with money and organizational leadership. But there was always the need for sustained, capable, concerned lay leadership from the outside—the suburbs—for the ablest people living in the inner city do not live there long. They leave as soon as they can; and therefore the question of lay leadership in the Christian congregation in the inner city is a chronic problem.

Some people in Aldersgate Church became concerned about the inner city. Speakers came to describe the conditions and needs there. Paul Younger, minister of the Fidelity Baptist Church, one of the churches of the Inner City Parish, on one occasion emphasized the need for suburban laymen to become involved personally in the work. However, at that time no one came forth to offer himself. The church did begin to send a sum of money annually to aid the inner-city work.

But one autumn evening a group of young couples gathered to help the people of Fidelity Baptist Church paint several Sunday school rooms in their church building. The membership of Fidelity is about 80 per cent Negro, and most of the people who worked with the Aldersgate couples that night were Negroes. It was a fruitful evening of labor and fellowship, and a seed of concern began to grow in the hearts of a few.

One of the Aldersgate Church men in this group of painters was especially sensitive to human suffering. His youth had been filled with tragedy. His only brother had committed suicide at the age of twenty-four. His mother endured prolonged suffering with a disease that finally caused her death after more than ten years of agony. He was bitter and had resigned himself to the meaninglessness of human existence. Upon graduation from college, he came to Cleveland to work as a research chemist. A friend invited him to go to church one Sunday, and in order to be a "good guy," he went along. He felt strangely moved during the service, the first that he had attended in a long time and decided to come back the next Sunday. Soon he found himself worshiping regularly. A few months later he was married. He writes,

My wife and I decided to join the church and began to go to the membership classes. I was floored! We were actually told that we had to go to church every Sunday, support the church financially, work on one of the church commissions, and even read the Bible! We joined the church anyway. I began to work with the church-sponsored Boy Scout troop. At the urging of the minister, my wife and I decided to join a *koinonia* group. We were encouraged to discover that other people in this group had doubts, disbeliefs, and questions too.

Relationships in that group deepened rapidly. It happened that four of the five couples in the group lived on the same block. As their study progressed, they discussed the relevance of Christian faith to the matter of housing segregation. They agreed that such segregation was unchristian and that they would be willing to have Negroes in their block. Not long after, the strong possibility arose that a Negro would buy a house two houses from the home of a group member. They encouraged the homeowner and assured him that they would stay and welcome a Negro family if the home were sold to one. This momentary neighborhood crisis was a revelation to the young man of whom I have been writing, even though the house eventually was not bought by a Negro. The man writes,

This was the first time that I consciously realized that I was somehow different from what I had been, for before these months of sharing in our *koinonia* group, I would not have taken this stand on the integration issue. Under this confrontation I began to see that my friends in the group were also changing. None of them had had a dramatic conversion to Christ. Rather, they had moved slowly through their own particular darkness into the light. I too had been moving about in the darkness and never recognized that I was approaching light. When I saw my friends "finding Christ," I realized that Christ had found me too. I felt like getting up and telling the world! Sunday worship and *koinonia* meetings became filled with deeper meaning. The petty problems of my work, home life, and personal finances were reduced to nothing when compared to the suffering and need of the world. I felt compelled to serve.

So it happened that this man telephoned me one day and asked if there was a need for Scout leaders in the Inner City Parish. When I called Paul Younger to inquire about such a need, he said, "Why this is tremendous, marvelous; the only Scout leader worth anything down here has left the community, and our Scouting program has ground to a halt. We desperately need experienced leadership." The man conferred with Paul Younger, and within a matter of weeks the Scouting program at Fidelity Baptist Church was resumed under the leadership of three Aldersgate men, all members of the *koinonia* group described above. Thus a seed of mission was germinated which was to bear fruit beyond the capacity of our imagination. Christian mission is born when God brings together the fertile soil of human need and the creative seed of a man's compassion. Christ takes shape in that need and that compassion, and the church becomes a servant people.

The three suburban laymen met with the Inner City troop committee to discuss the situation and to assure them of their own continuing commitment to stay and see the program through. Gradually the number of youngsters involved grew from ten to over twenty. A few parents began to take an interest and to believe that the white suburbanites really wanted to help them! At the end of February that year the troop held its first camp-out, an experience that greatly increased the morale of the Scouts. In March two committeemen from among the parents of the inner-city boys volunteered to become Scout leaders. The suburban laymen worked with them and prepared them to take over the leadership of the troop. In May an exchange basketball game was held at Fidelity with the suburban Troop 210 of Warrensville Heights. Fidelity won. During the summer, camp-outs were held with joint participation of suburban and inner-city troops. The walls of class, race, culture, and geography that separate Christ's people were beginning to shake just a little.

In the spring of that year a retreat was held for fifteen Aldersgate women concerning the mission of the suburban church to the city. It was led by Betty Younger, wife of the minister of Fidelity Baptist Church. The women discovered how naïve and uninformed they were about the city at whose edge they lived. The were overwhelmed by Mrs. Younger's statistics pertaining to the slum area that surrounds Fidelity Church, where 85,000 people live in two square miles of territory, 40 per cent of them children under the age of five. Incomes range downward from $8000 annually to what is derived from relief. The reason for the wide discrepancy in income is that those who can afford better housing have few places to go because most suburbs do not want Negroes and find ways to prevent them from buying suburban homes. Ghetto living, schools on relay session, inadequate police protection, chronic unemployment—all these aspects of slum existence were present, as they are in every major metropolitan area in the country. One of the women wrote,

The whole retreat was an eye-opening experience. It strengthened our growing conviction that some of us must join our husbands in the mission to the Inner City. We asked what we could do and were invited to participate personally in needed work at Fidelity Church. We became Associate Members of Fidelity Church, which is a relationship available to members of other churches who wish to help in the work of Fidelity.

The first task of these women was to help with an unemployment survey currently being conducted by members of Fidelity. The survey had been requested by congressmen from the area in the hope that its findings would assist them in determining ways to combat the chronic unemployment of the residents. The women worked side by side with Fidelity members and were brought right into the homes of the neighborhood. They saw for the first time with their own eyes the effect of months of unemployment—hopelessness, the gradual loss of initiative, surrender. They saw families living on Aid to Dependent Children funds. Statistics were suddenly transformed into suffering human beings. A woman wrote,

One day we met Pat. When her husband died, she was left with six children and no income. We first met the family when Pat needed transportation to the hospital to visit her two-month-old, seven-pound baby who was near death from malnutrition. As we entered her home, her two-year-old baby peeked at us as he hung way out of the second-story window. There was no glass in either the front- or back-door window. The house had a not-so-sweet-smelling odor, and an oil burner in the living room had an open flame accessible to any of the children. We stayed with the children that morning while their mother went to the hospital to visit, and we heard the rest of the story. The two-year-old had had a very bad case of pneumonia as an infant and looked as though he also had had rickets. The three-year-old had had lead poisoning from eating plaster and paint. From the brain damage that resulted she often goes into convulsions. . . . None of the children had shoes that fit. Pat herself has high blood pressure and naturally feels weak much of the time. This is what the social workers type as a multiple-problem case! Aside from all their problems, however, the children were very well mannered and showed much love for one another. On our second visit when we told her how nice her children were, Pat said, "I can't give my kids much; but I can still give them love." This really struck us, for often in our striving to give our children material comforts, we forget that above all they need our love.

From their involvement in this survey, the women moved to meet other needs. A sewing class was set up at Fidelity that summer under the leadership of two Aldersgate women.

As both men and women became more deeply committed to the work in the inner city, they thought of starting a *koinonia* group with some of their Fidelity friends. A group composed of three

Fidelity couples and seven people from Aldersgate was organized. Using *The Bible Speaks To You*[1] as their text, this group shared discussion, prayer, and personal experience. Rapidly they reached a level of honesty and personal sharing deeper than that achieved in the groups in which the Aldersgate members had previously participated. And how could it have been otherwise! For obviously the only motivation for these diverse people to come together was their common faith in Jesus Christ. They discovered that their differences of background, outlook, and color, which had been factors of alienation and distrust, could become sources of mutual enrichment. They began to know that unity in Christ of which Paul speaks: "There is neither Jew nor Greek, there is neither slave nor free, there is neither male nor female; for you are all one in Christ Jesus" (Gal. 3:28, 29). Out of this group developed the most exciting and significant venture of the mission to the inner city—the most exciting venture to date, it must be added, for God has a way of bringing ever fresh surprises out of His servant people. This venture has come to be known as The Outpost.

It rapidly became evident to the members of this group that a concrete form of communication needed to be established between the suburbs and the inner city. Lack of suburban understanding of city problems suggested the possibility of some sort of communication outpost in the suburban community that would dramatize the suburban church's responsibility for the needs of the city and would serve as a tangible symbol of awakening concern for the city. It was decided that The Outpost should be located outside a church building, perhaps in a shopping center, in order to demonstrate that the church belongs in the world rather than inside its own four walls. In addition, physical separation from denominational structures would facilitate the interdenominational, as well as interracial, character of the experiment and would assure additional financial support from other churches and individuals. In the beginning it was hoped that Aldersgate Church and the Inner City Parish would finance the project.

The Outpost would be a center of information for both urban and suburban communities, concerning such problems as employment, education, welfare, urban renewal, political action, volunteer community programs—Boy Scouts, United Appeal, etc.—hospitals and clinics, housing, alcoholism, and juvenile delinquency. It would also provide suitable facilities for the collection of food and used clothing for city churches and materials for Goodwill Industries, or a secretarial service to urban and suburban churches, for a meeting place for noon prayer groups and other interdenominational groups, and for an outlet for the products of the home industries of members of city churches. An additional source of income would derive from the sale of religious books. The hope was that many concerned people in the Cleveland area would buy their religious books from The Outpost.

At first The Outpost was to be operated by a volunteer staff of people from the suburbs and the city. The volunteer staff consisted at that time of the *koinonia* group of people from Aldersgate and Fidelity Baptist. Appropriately, therefore, it was an interracial, interdenominational structure within two local congregations that gave birth to The Outpost. The role of the suburban churches was conceived initially as that of using The Outpost for experimental projects seeking to establish closer urban-suburban relationships and providing financial and personnel assistance. The role of the inner-city churches was understood to be that of disseminating information to the suburban churches regarding the city's problems, employment needs and opportunities, activities at the center, etc., so that this information could be relayed from The Outpost to all city churches.

Eventually The Outpost would lead, hopefully, to the establishment of a Retreat House on the edge of the inner-city area of Cleveland. Such a House could serve as a fellowship, study, and work center for suburban and urban Christians in a nonchurch setting. It was a vision of providing for inner-city people something of a retreat from their asphalt jungle existence, close enough in time and distance to make it feasible. The Retreat House would welcome non-Christians and seek to appeal to the unchurched by genuine identification with them and concrete services to them.

But let us return for the present to the development of The Outpost itself. With great hope and much prayer, the project was presented to the Official Board of Aldersgate Church by the minister, Alan Davis. It was unanimously approved, with a pledge of $650 for the beginning months of its operation. After considerable searching, a storefront was located in a suburban shopping center. It had a tiny conference room, two offices, and a lounge. On one side was a building company; on the other, a restaurant. It was cleaned and a few sticks of furniture were installed. With the prayers of the wider Christian community and the curiosity of many others, The Outpost was opened and dedicated on September 30, 1962.

The church had established a new kind of beachhead in the world. The statement on the pamphlet describing The Outpost reads:

This Outpost is an inter-denominational, inter-racial link between city and suburbs. That's our definition. The Outpost is an experiment, an effort by churchmen to share the responsibility for the problems of the inner city. The Outpost is not an end in itself. It is a small way to dramatize the need for the church to reach out into the world. It may not work. Our ideas are untested. But it is a beginning.

During the first year of operation The Outpost proved itself a significant bridge between suburban and inner-city Christians. Dozens of job requests and referrals have been made. Large quantities of food and clothing have been received and personally delivered to needy people. Increasing numbers of invitations come to the volunteers who staff The Outpost to describe its work to groups in urban and suburban churches in the Cleveland area. Dialogue groups involving clergy and laymen from all over the city have begun to meet at The Outpost. It is becoming an effective focus of Christian responsibility for the metropolitan area.

The structure altered somewhat during the first year of operation. The Outpost was incorporated, with a Board of Trustees consisting of ten people—two from Aldersgate, two from Fidelity Baptist, and six concerned persons from other churches. Book sales provided only a small, though valuable, part of the cost of operation. Aldersgate Church pledged an additional $600 for the coming year and other monies were pledged by the Inner City Parish. New sources of revenue were explored, to make the financial support as broad as possible. Many concerned churches and individuals contributed to the $1500-plus budget.

It was clear that the inner city is as valid a missionary field as any in the modern world, and that such a venture as The Outpost requires and merits the support of concerned denominational boards, congregations, and individuals. In the years ahead many churches and persons will want to include, in their benevolent giving, money to be devoted to the support of such courageous unconventional ministries.[2]

The Kingdom of God always begins small. Consider Mark 30:32:

And he said, "With what can we compare the kingdom of God, or what parable shall we use for it? It is like a grain of mustard seed, which, when sown upon the ground, is the smallest of all the seeds on earth; yet when it is sown it grows up and becomes the greatest of all shrubs, and puts forth large branches, so that the birds of the air can make nests in its shade."

So it is when two or three are gathered in Christ's name to be His servants in the service of men. Their work is important in itself. But it also dramatically symbolizes, to those both inside and outside the church who are touched by it, what the church is called to be, all the time, in every place, for every member. It is not merely the chance whim of a few, but defines the discipleship and apostleship conferred upon *all* who would take the name of Christ. One concrete picture of the church as Christ's servant in the world is worth more than many books and sermons on the subject.

In every local church there are persons in whom the seed of mission is waiting to be born. Around every local church, and especially all churches located in or near metropolitan areas, there is human misery crying out for help. People who are given eyes to see will see the need to which they are being called. People who are given ears to hear will hear the voices of need calling to them. A local church, by God's grace, may let a small part of its corporate life be infiltrated by the seed of mission. No one can tell how that seed will grow, what old structures in that church will be broken as the new life enlarges and strains for form and expression. Each concrete situation will be different. But there are common factors that usually emerge as a local church becomes a servant people.

1. *Mission is born in* koinonia. Rarely does a person burst forth in personal mission who has not first been awakened and nourished by the beloved fellowship. The story of the call about Scouting in the inner city, which ultimately resulted in The Outpost, is a case in point. Persons must first be found before they can go out and find. Persons must first be served before they know what it means to be a servant. This is to say, the church must first *be* the church in its own inner life before it can begin to *be* the church in the world. A missionary church has first been a ministering church. An apostle is one who was first a disciple. This is what makes Christian service different from humanitarian service. Christian servants go into the world to serve because Christ first served and loved them. Before there will be new life in the world, there must be new life in the church.

2. *Mission is born in the heart of one person at a time.* Our time schedule matters nothing; it is only in the fullness of God's time that the seed of mission is germinated. A minister or layman cannot force or push a mission concern on another person. Mission comes to the surface from inner pressure; it can never be imposed by any kind of outer pressure, whether applied by minister, bishop, board, or committee. God gives a man his peculiar call to concrete servanthood. The Outpost began in the compassionate

hope of one man, who wrote to me at the beginning of the venture, "We are only a handful of people with no funds but with Jesus Christ. The odds are in our favor!" So they are! So it was in the days of the New Testament church.

3. *Mission reaches to "the least of these."* Jesus pictured the final judgment of God in terms of man's compassionate service to the stranger, the hungry, sick, imprisoned, and naked; Christ's church is sent to serve "the least of these." George Webber writes,

"This special service of the church has to be a *help of the helpless.*" It is the special function of the church always to be on the alert and to pray to God that she may really see the helpless people of our day and then have the courage to take up the task of service which is demanded.[3]

Every local church will find its primary mission field in its own neighborhood, which, in a suburban setting, reaches from the church doors to the heart of the inner city in or near which the church people live. If we look out upon the city and listen, the city will tell us its needs and show us its helpless.

4. *The mission structures will be ecumenical and unconventional.* It is not coincidental that The Outpost is interdenominational and that it is located outside the walls of a church building. This is the time for ecumenical wineskins, the new wineskins. The Spirit, who calls us to unity, forces us to look for unifying structures. The Christ who sends us into the world forces us to dwell in the world as He did. This is the time when we must show the world that we, the church, are not an introverted community seeking to exalt our own parochial concerns. We must appear in new and arresting shapes, surprising that world which supposed that it knew the church and had already dismissed us as dull, utterly predictable, and smelling of stale piety. It is a time of mobility and daring, a time for going out, like

Abraham, not knowing where we are to go. It is a time for faith and hope and love.

5. *Suburban or urban captivity can be broken.* Gibson Winter's *Suburban Captivity of the Churches*[4] is a chilling documentation of the cultural and geographical captivity of Protestant churches located in the suburbs. He demonstrates that the principle of coming together in the suburbs is economic. People worship together because they can afford the same sized and priced house and thus live in the same neighborhood. They are isolated from those who are different—different economically, racially, culturally, and often ethnically. Therefore, the church, which by its very nature and essence is *inclusive,* is given an *exclusive* structure holding it fast and preventing it from being a real fellowship in Christ. We are discovering that in small but significant ways, such as are described in this and the following chapter, suburban captivity can be broken through. All that is needed is one servant of Christ. Others will be found. Bridges can be built between inner city and suburb, white and Negro, rich and poor. The forms these bridges take will vary in the variety of situations. Perhaps some persons will become associate members of inner-city churches. Perhaps some urban or suburban church will accept a measure of financial integration of resources to meet the total needs of two parishes. Perhaps some persons in suburban churches will feel the need to become full members of an inner-city church. And a few may find themselves uprooting their families from the suburbs and returning to live in the city. There is hope in the most encrusted of traditional churches, in the most conservative and myopic of people. For the Holy Spirit blows where He wills, and He may will to blow upon even us and our people and our minister!

6. *The "far off" and the "near" need each other.* Paul writes in Ephesians 2:13-17 of the uniting of Gentile and Jew, who had been separated but now are brought together in Christ:

But now in Christ Jesus you who once were far off [the Gentile] have been brought near in the blood of Christ. For he is our peace, who has made us both one, and has broken down the dividing wall of hostility . . . that he might create in himself one new man in place of the two, so making peace, and might reconcile us both to God in one body through the cross, thereby bringing the hostility to an end. And he came and preached peace to you who were far off and peace to those who were near.

Paul is saying that those who are separated from one another by dividing walls of hostility—walls of race, religion, culture, or wealth—are brought together in Christ, in the church which is His body. Therefore, we come to understand that the suburban white cannot *be* fully reconciled to Christ without the inner-city Negro. We belong to Him by belonging to one another. The highly cultured and educated person of privilege cannot fully plumb the depths of Christ's empowering fellowship unless he is enabled to share Christ with the uncultured, uneducated person of little privilege. In whatever ways a local church is segmented economically, politically, or socially, it is to that extent an attenuated version of the church. What we know in such a situation is not full fellowship in Christ but the particular delights of cultural customs and traditions that can smother the church in a given place and time.

One night some years ago, one hundred people of Aldersgate Church and one hundred people of Parkwood Methodist Church (Negro) gathered for an evening of fellowship and worship together. Few who were there will ever forget it. These congregations had shared annual exchanges of worship for some years, and in other ways had sought to work together from time to time. We gathered for supper in the Fellowship Hall of Aldersgate Church. We came together as families and sat at table together. It had been planned carefully that an Aldersgate and a Parkwood family would share the same table. The families of both ministers sat together. Conversation was slow at the beginning but grew in quality and meaning toward the end of the meal. We began to sing. One of the four sons of the Parkwood minister sang a solo in his boy's voice, a sweet soprano, and the assembly was visibly moved. We sang spirituals, and in the singing there came a swelling awareness that we were truly God's people *together*.

We moved to the sanctuary for a brief time of worship. Scripture was read by laymen of both churches. There was singing of hymns. Then the two ministers walked to the center of the chancel before the altar and the cross, and with hands clasped together each in turn prayed. It seemed to many that these clasped hands symbolized the "one new man" created by Christ out of our diversity, the uniting of those far off and near. The "gospel" truth is that *we need each other*. Let the suburb reach to the inner city, and let the inner city reach to the suburb. Let those who are "different" find their union together in Christ.

Chapter 5

The Witnessing Community

. . . Be ready at any time to give a quiet and
reverent answer to any man who wants a reason for
the hope that you have within you.

I Peter 3:15, *Phillips*

A servant people inevitably becomes a witnessing community.
When we identify ourselves with the sufferings of others who
have no observable claim on us, the world takes note. When our
concern to serve the helpless, and the least of these, takes the
shape of personal involvement in his need, the world looks at us.
The servant people, identified with those whom they came to
serve, are suddenly visible. The leaven which was hid cannot be
concealed any longer; the light is seen to be shining in the darkness; there is a community as obvious as a city set on a hill.

The Outpost is one visible sign of a servant people become a
witnessing community. Just by being what it is and where it is,
The Outpost is an occasion which makes the world curious.
People come and ask what it is, and why it is there, and just who
is—and what is the real angle—behind it. Suddenly the world is
at its doors asking the "reason for the hope" that is inside.

What does it mean to be a witnessing community? What is the
shape of our witness? We will be dealing in this chapter with our

contextual witness, that word and deed which arise out of the context of our servanthood when people ask us questions of faith. This is not a "telling" witness so much as an "answering" witness. This is not witness in terms of our imposition of faith upon an uninterested world; it is witness in terms of our response to a world made curious by the shape of our service. The witnessing community arises from the life of a servant people, as the possibility of reconciliation arises out of the reality of incarnation. When we incarnate the "ministry of reconciliation" (II Cor. 5:18), we are sometimes asked to give the "message of reconciliation" (II Cor. 5:19).

Three women in a prayer group were seeking some concrete way to serve a real need in the community. They wanted something beyond ministry within the church and family. They heard that there was a need for volunteers in a canteen at the Highland View Hospital, a hospital for the chronically ill, located on the southeastern edge of Cleveland. On several nights a week volunteer groups open and staff a canteen which otherwise could not be open because of the prohibitive costs of operating it with paid labor. As the women made arrangements to inquire about the canteen work, an article appeared in the newspaper about a movie made at the hospital portraying the rehabilitation of a typical patient.

The movie was obtained for a general meeting of the Woman's Society of the church, and a nurse came from the hospital to tell its story. She described the great need not only for volunteer staffing of the canteen, but also for help with feeding some of the patients, who because of their illness could not feed themselves. A large number of the patients in the hospital were in advanced stages of multiple sclerosis, a disease which affects the nervous system and leaves the victim immobile physically, but alert mentally. The women decided that they would staff the canteen two nights a week, and that a few of them would also help in feeding the patients.

The three women who had initiated the project were interviewed by hospital authorities and supplied with the rules and regulations of volunteer work. After touring the hospital, and hearing of the desperate need for helpers in a section where the patients were beyond hope of getting well, they decided to begin feeding there. At first they expected to feed a large number of patients in their weekly visits. One of them writes,

But it didn't take long for us to realize the difference in what the hospital expected—the simple feeding of a patient—and what we felt called to do. What started out to be feeding patients soon turned into ministering to their deeper needs, reaching out to them in love, taking the time really to be concerned for them as persons. For these patients are the "forgotten people," forgotten by their families and friends who after several years begin to tire of visiting and sometimes come only once or twice a year! They suffer not only from bodily sickness, but sickness of heart. They know the fellowship of the lonely.

Feeding grew into writing letters and dressing hair, to reading, to listening and sharing. Countless small personal ministries were offered and gratefully received. All the while, deeper relationships were developing between the women from Aldersgate and their patients. Confronted with real suffering of a kind that makes the irritations and complaints of ordinary society seem meaningless, the Aldersgate women discovered a new personal freedom. Again, one of them writes,

Most of the patients have nothing to hide and have long since laid aside the layers of pretense which obscured their true selves. They don't realize that their own personal openness leaves the doors open for us to lay aside our pretenses, enabling us more truly to show and share our love for them. With them we are enabled to forget ourselves and be wholly natural. Strangely, through their sickness we have been given a kind of healing and health of spirit ourselves. We know, of course, that they give much more to us than we can possibly give to them, because they give out of their poverty all they can give . . . themselves.

Genuine Christian servanthood characteristically results in the creation of fellowship. The server and the served begin to see each other as persons, and a mutual ministry is born which could

not have been anticipated. "It is impossible to express the true
meaning of this ministry without experiencing it personally,"
observes one woman. The original three began to meet on Saturday afternoon at the church for a period of quiet and prayer
together before going to minister at Highland View. This time of
preparation became a very important part of their total mission.
It was a time not only to pray for their patient-friends at the
hospital, but also to receive the tranquility and peace required to
minister to them. In another letter,

> We know that ministering without personal communication is not
> ministry but only busywork and time-serving. Instead of arriving at
> the hospital at full speed ready to rush through our work, we are
> enabled to come with the inner control that prayer brings.

The question is sometimes asked, "What is the difference between volunteer service and being a servant Christian?" There
is no longer any question in our minds that there *is* a difference.
To know this ourselves is a joy; to be able to describe and mark
out the "difference" is difficult, because we are dealing with convictions and motivations which are often hidden. In addition, it
is unhealthy to be taking one's spiritual pulse, attempting to ascer-
tain how we may be different from (not better than) others with
a genuine concern. On the other hand, we should not be immobil-
ized by self-consciousness, for we need to understand that as
Christians we do what we do in Christ's name and for His sake.

Here is the "difference" between a volunteer and a servant
Christian. The servant Christian is also a Christian witness. The
form of a servant is his appropriate context for a responsive
witness. When the world is served in Christian love, the world
itself raises the questions of faith. The Christian who, chronolog-
ically speaking, is first a servant finds his opportunity for witness
precisely in the relationships created by his servanthood. It is the
servant who is called upon "to give the reason for the hope that is
within" (I Pet. 3:15, Phillips). Here are two examples in which
the "difference," the witness, begins to take shape.

The first concerns Mary, a multiple-sclerosis patient at Highland View Hospital. She was completely paralyzed from her neck down. At times she had difficulty eating. When she was tense she could scarcely speak at all, and it was very hard to understand what she was saying. She had been at Highland View ten years and was now forty-two years old. She had a son, thirteen, who was in an orphanage, and a husband, who came to see her twice a year. She had no way of communicating with them apart from their visits. Mary had come to hate her husband because of the way he ignored her. She had turned inward and become so silent that the nurses wondered whether she had lost her capacity to speak. One of the Aldersgate women began to feed her and describes the relationship which emerged:

After reassuring her that we would be there to feed her every Saturday night, and after weeks of doing it, she began to show some signs of interest in us. And the first word she spoke to us was my name, "Ruth." Mary began to open up and talk about her fears and disbeliefs. She did not want material help but encouragement and talk. We had the feeling that she had not really conversed with anyone in years, chiefly because there was no one to listen to her and take the trouble to understand what she was trying to say, brokenly and with great effort. When a relationship of real trust was established, we were able to talk with her of prayer and its importance for her as her real contact with the world. She began to see that she was still needed and useful, for she could pray! We shared with her the life of our church, the failures and the victories. We told her of persons and situations in need of her prayers. In truth, we could almost watch her beginning to "live" again. Her physical condition is not better—even worse. But she doesn't lie and cry the hours away as she did in the past. She knows that we pray for her every day. We have spoken to her of the Resurrection and she understands, believes, and is comforted.

This patient not only has received an external physical service but has been embraced by a living community of faith, literally loved back into a significant life. She has come to have some insight into the meaning of her suffering and has been enabled to be a person with a worthy gift to give the world through prayer. The servant people were asked to become the witnessing community by the one whom they were serving. When the world receives a valid ministry of reconciliation, the world wants to hear the message of reconciliation, but from the lips of those who minister. It is the deed which makes possible the word, the service which is the cradle for witness.

The second example of how the specifically Christian witness takes shape concerns a patient named Gertrude. She had more visitors than the other patients in her room, and it seemed as though she was the least in need of the personal ministries of the Aldersgate women. But Gertrude was curious and forever asking questions about Aldersgate. On one of my own visits to Highland View Hospital I stopped briefly in the room where Gertrude and three other patients lived. During a short conversation with her, she said to me, "The Aldersgate women are unique. Practically my whole life now is dependent upon volunteers, and I know that there is something different about the women from your church. They care for us more than the members of our own families."

The occasion for Christian witness was not long in coming. One of our women writes,

It happened that Christmas Eve was on a Saturday, so Christmas Eve we were at the hospital feeding. Gertrude remarked to me, "You're all lit up tonight!" And so I was! I was so filled with love for her and the others that Christmas Eve. This was not the pity that I used to feel for people who weren't able to share the "mad flurry" of Christmas Eve, but the love that only Christ can fill us with. I was grateful to be with her at a time which, in other years, had been the busiest and most harried night of the year. Gertrude could see the deep joy I felt in ministering to her. And when she spoke to me, I prayed that the radiance of God's love in Christ would never be taken from me.

I told her quite simply about Christ. From then on it was easy to share with Gertrude, even though she was of Jewish faith. Many times I wondered how much of my Christian faith she could accept. Could she really believe that it was Christ's love that sent us out there? We never learned, because after fifteen years of lying paralyzed in that hospital bed, Gertrude died. It almost seemed to me as if our fellowship with her during the last year of her life was a kind of preparation for what was to come. On the night she died I prayed for her, and as nearly as I can remember, it was like this: "O God, Gertrude is with Thee and can now know Christ fully and be able to accept Him. Now she can understand the times when I shared with her what His love meant to me. Thank you, Lord!"

When the "light that enlightens every man" (John 1:9) begins to shine in us, people see it and want to know what it is and where it comes from. And we are then able to tell them whose light it is. We are willing to wait a long time for the privilege of this kind of witness. We are also willing to accept *not* having the privilege if the door is not opened to us. But we are ready and expectant and prayerful, knowing that the day and hour when the Lord comes is always near at hand.

From these concrete examples perhaps we can generalize concerning the "difference" between humanitarian services and the witness of a Christian servant. There are at least three distinctive aspects of the shape of Christian service.

1. *Motivation.* One may do "good deeds" for a variety of motives. A humanist may be motivated by his reverence for and gratitude to life itself. The Christian servant is motivated by his reverence for and gratitude to the Lord of life, Jesus Christ. It is the knowledge of Christ's love that drives a Christian servant to serve others as Christ has served him (John 13:1-15). The humanist may indeed be a superlative person with great compassion. But only the Christian goes forth because he has been sent by Christ, to offer the love of Christ. "Evangelism consists of loving another human being in a way which represents to him the care of God for his particular life. . . . Evangelism is the event in which a Christian confronts another man in a way which assures the other man that the new life which he observes in the Christian is vouchsafed for him also."[1]

2. *Resources.* The humanist brings the depth of his own concern. The Christian servant comes primarily not in his own strength but in the strength of Christ. The Christian servant, and

only he, can point to Christ, who is the hope of finding meaning in suffering that is beyond stoic endurance. The Christian can bring the promise of resurrection, and the living hope of an inheritance which "nothing can destroy or spoil or wither" (I Pet. 1:4, NEB).

3. *Fellowship.* The humanist comes by himself, speaks for himself, and offers his own services. The Christian servant comes as a representative of a witnessing community, a corporate life that includes him but goes far beyond him, that bears him up and gives him power and joy. The fact that there are, at any one time, several Aldersgate people engaged in this ministry together is dramatic expression of the truth that the *church* is there in their servanthood. The possibility of sharing in the community of faith, through this kind of conversation and in wider fashion through prayer, is something only the Christian brings.

Changes take place in those Christian witnesses that are sometimes highly visible to those who know them well. Their friends and family can see something new happening in them, interpret it as they will. One of the women serving at Highland View wrote of another woman also serving there:

She reveals in herself what is in many women—a desire for creative ministry beyond that which can be found in home and family life, and the usual activities of a church. This concern to serve often is hidden in the "good works" of a church bazaar, a PTA project, or something similar. I have watched her find in her personal ministry at Highland View the creative outlet for Christ's love in her which has really released her as a person, and given her a context for true compassion instead of only time consumption. All she needed was someone who really needed her and others to go with her. She has been enabled to give herself in a creatively Christian manner as never before.

The witnessing community continues to live at Highland View Hospital. Scores of women have served in the canteen, at first staffed on Wednesday night, and then also on Saturday. Personal contact in feeding patients taught the Aldersgate women that the canteen could be a great opportunity for fellowship with patients as well as just a matter of making a sandwich or a cup of coffee. In fact, these little transactions could be the vehicle for the personal expression of interest and concern. Saturday nights, when few visitors or members of the hospital staff are present, offer a more quiet and relaxed opportunity for personal conversation and fellowship.

Because of the desire of the patients for more such fellowship, the idea of a recreation center was born, a place to play games of various kinds with those patients able to do so. The suggestion was at first vetoed by the hospital administration because of the supposed necessity for a supervisor in the event of practical or personal emergencies. But finally permission was given to use a room off the main corridor on the first floor for playing cards, checkers, etc. A few men began to accompany their wives on Thursday nights to the Recreation Center. Sometimes there was a community sing. The Center represents another context in which Christian love can be shared. Here the church is planted in the world in a nonchurch setting. Here is the environment in which we are asked again and again to "give the reason for the hope that is within" (I Pet. 3:15, Phillips). Here is a beachhead of hope in a country of despair, still another form of the witnessing community.

"I was sick and you visited me" (Matt. 25:36). What a wealth of hope and possibility lies in those words! There is some community of sick people near any local church awaiting the ministry of servant Christians. Perhaps it is an ordinary hospital, or a mental hospital, or a school for retarded children, or a home for the aged, or a prison, or a workhouse. The varieties of human sickness and sorrow are many. The context of our servant witness will always be different and the regulations of the host institution will vary. But in every such place, for those who look and listen, there is the need for personal ministry. Why do we ministers and laymen wait so long to recognize the least of these near our churches? Why did it take us at Aldersgate more than six years to become sufficiently concerned to reach into the inner city and

into Highland View Hospital? Perhaps more than our blindness
and sin is involved. Perhaps it is also a question of the fullness of
God's time. And it is certain that the fullness of His time has come
or is coming soon in the lives of untold churches and individuals
in countless corners of our world. " 'And behold, I am coming
soon.' . . . Amen. Come, Lord Jesus!" (Rev. 22:7, 20).

PART II. *Reshaping the Christian Life*

Chapter 6

Awareness of Forgiveness

> *For the love of Christ leaves us no choice, when
> once we have reached the conclusion that one man
> died for all and therefore all mankind has died. His
> purpose in dying for all was that men, while still in
> life, should cease to live for themselves, and should live
> for him who for their sake died and was raised to life.*
>
> *II Corinthians 5:14, 15, NEB*

As the church begins to take the shape of Christ in the ways appropriate to its particular mission, the individual Christian in the congregation finds his own life being reshaped. He discovers his own identity in the community which knows itself to be the family of Christ and the army of the Lord. He discovers his own vocation in the fellowship which knows itself to be a servant people and a witnessing community. In the chapters that follow we will explore the ways Christ takes shape in the individual as the One who *forgives* him, commissions him an agent of reconciliation, sets him free to walk in the Spirit, and orders his living. The process begins with an awareness of forgiveness.

One evening my wife and I were in a restaurant listening to a gifted pianist and his instrumental group. There was feeling, artistry, rich chording, delight, and devotion in his playing. We were grateful to be there listening and sharing the joy of his music. Midway through the evening, three women came into the restaurant and were seated at a table near ours. As soon as they sat down, one of them started talking to the other two, compulsively, persistently, so busily wrapped up in her own chatter that she utterly missed the creative thing that was happening as the pianist played. She was there, her ears were in good physical condition so far as could be told, but she did not hear. She was deaf to the sound of beauty. I half turned to stare at her with anger for a moment, not catching her eye because her eye never left her two immediate victims. Then it struck me that she was also cheapening me and involving me so that I too was no longer hearing the music. I turned back, thinking how sad and damnable it is that we get so bent inward to ourselves that we become unaware of beauty, of other persons, of the presence of God.

Hell is total preoccupation with self. Hell is the condition of being tone deaf to the word of grace, blind to the presence of God, unable to discern His image in another person. Hell is that state in which we no longer catch the fragrance of life or breathe in the salt breeze of the Holy Spirit; when the taste buds of life are so dulled that there is no tang or sparkle to living. Hell is to live in the presence of love and not know it, not feel it, not be warmed by it. It is to live in the Father's house like the older son (Luke 15) but be insensitive to the Father's love. Hell is to be unaware of God's world, God's people, the reality of God in oneself; it is to have the doors in life closed tight, to abide in one's own darkness.

Some time ago a letter came to me from a college student, in which she spoke of her experience of darkness:

I guess it is not at all hard for us to magnify our own particular difficulties until they seem to envelop us and we shut everyone and everything else out of the picture and dwell only upon ourselves. I realized during worship Wednesday night that I have been present in the midst of Christ's work, even participating in it, and yet somehow I have shut Him out for myself. I do not know how it is that one can feel very close to God, as I once did when I was just entering high school, and yet live on and gradually grow away from Him. But it happened to me.

It happens to many of us who grow up in the church and are members of it. We who at one time were close to God become preoccupied with our careers, and God begins to fade from our consciousness. We may be busily participating in the activity of the church and yet somehow in the very business shut Christ out in terms of any personal knowledge of His presence in our lives. The tragedy of the modern church is that we have become distracted by our serving, like Martha, and do not know how to see and hear and know the Lord Himself. Millions of modern church members nibble at the husk of the church's life but never find the food and drink of the living Christ. Thus, as the years pass, we go through the forms of faith and worship and take comfort in our religious routine. But all the while we remain unchanged and unchanging, our ideas rigidly locked in place, our spirits drooping like our sagging bodies, dying literally while yet in life, knowing little either of guilt or of grace, unaware of the living God in our midst. How can we come into a new and vital knowledge of God?

The dawn breaks when we become personally aware of God's forgiveness. Paul describes this central event which makes a man a Christian: "For the love of Christ leaves us no choice, when once we have reached the conclusion that one man died for all and therefore all mankind has died. His purpose in dying for all was that men, while still in life, should cease to live for themselves, and should live for him who for their sake died and was raised to life" (II Cor. 5:14, 15, NEB). It is one thing to know with my mind that God forgives men their sins, and quite another to become aware of God's forgiveness of *my* sins. It is one thing to know that God so loved the world that He gave His Son, but quite another to realize that God so loved *me* that He gave His Son. When I hear the gospel in the first person singular addressed to me, then contact is made, the general becomes particular, something breaks into life in me. It is a matter of recognition and awareness.

It was when the Prodigal Son "came to himself" (Luke 15:17)

and returned to the father who loved him that he received forgiveness and new life could begin. In the awesome recognition
that the risen Christ had appeared first to him, Peter understood
the amazing forgiveness of the Lord he had denied and became
a new man. Paul could never forget that the risen Christ "appeared also to me" (I Cor. 15:8), the last and the least of the
apostles, the one who had been persecuting Him (Acts 9:4). It
was when Martin Luther perceived that he had but to throw
himself upon the mercy of a gracious God, without the torment
of recalling and confessing every single sin, that he became aware
of the depth and breadth of Christ's forgiveness and was able to
receive His freedom. John Wesley was a good man of God until,
in the context of a Bible Study Group meeting on May 24, 1738,
he became aware of Christ's forgiveness for *his* sins.

> About a quarter before nine, while he [the group leader] was
> describing the change which God works in the heart through faith in
> Christ, I felt my heart strangely warmed. I felt I did trust in Christ,
> Christ alone, for salvation; and an assurance was given me that He
> had taken away my sins, even mine. . . .[1]

Whether one becomes aware of Christ's forgiveness in a particular time and place which one can remember clearly or over a
period of many months, the forgiving love of God personally
offered through the death and resurrection of Christ remains the
same. Whether or not there is the feeling of a warmed heart is not
at issue. Rather, the essential thing is the personal conviction
shaped in the bedrock of a man's being that Christ has forgiven
him, that the love of God for all men has now come to *this* man.

One night I was canoeing on a lake. The moon was shining
gloriously. As I looked up at it, I marveled that it seemed to be
shining directly on me. Wherever that canoe went, still the moonlight followed me. Yet I knew that, at the very same time,
moonlight was shining directly at other people in different places
on the lake. Somehow here was light for all men and yet light for
each individual. So Christ's forgiving love, which streams from
the cross upon all men, is beamed directly at each of us.

The deepest and most chronic need of the human spirit is to be forgiven. The surface loneliness and estrangement which torture modern man indicate the separation of man from himself, his fellows, and God. A letter came to me recently from a friend:

What a year! We married my brother Marshall last fall, we had our baby Johnnie, Aunt Ida died, and Ron's father is dying in a nursing home. With the school referendum and the natural joys and sorrows of five children, I feel as if we're on a perpetual emotional jag. My next-door neighbor has kicked her teenage daughter out of the house and told her not to come back, and another neighbor and mother of four has had a nervous breakdown, and a friendly couple down the street have become alcoholics. What we need in this town is a good fire-eating preacher with wife to match to show us what the meaning of this crazy life is—and to preach forgiveness, forgiveness, forgiveness. Isn't it strange how everything seems to boil down either to being unable on one's own to forgive others, or to feeling guilty and unloved oneself?

In this letter lies a world of insight, for the knowledge of forgiveness is that saving knowledge which opens a new world of meaning and purpose. Only in the presence of One who loves us so much as to lay down His life for us are we able to let our pretensions fall away and stand in the light as sinners—forgiven sinners! Only when we become aware of forgiveness do we receive power to forgive others. The ability to forgive in Christ's fashion is not a natural endowment; it is a capacity nurtured within us only as we are forgiven by others who know Him and thus learn through them the meaning of Christ's forgiveness.

This is to say that the church of Christ must be a forgiven and a forgiving fellowship, the family in which we love one another as He has loved us and come to recognize one another as brothers and sisters. Awareness of Christ's forgiveness is the treasure hidden in the earthen vessel of His church. When we find that we forgive one another in His name, we share personally and fully His own forgiving love. We need to be forgiven; we need one another to be forgiven by Christ.

A little while ago I talked with a man who had been a "good church member" all his life and lived an exemplary business and social life. But for some reason he had never found the inner meaning and power promised by the New Testament. He felt somehow cheated and empty. He accepted an opportunity to study the Bible with a few others and entered with them upon a corporate search for truth and meaning in the New Testament. As these people became friends and began to share their experiences as well as their ideas, the tempo of the man's questions accelerated, a light came into his face, and I could almost watch the scales dropping from his eyes. He was "getting it"; or it was "getting through" to him. Over a period of some months a crucial realization and turning point had come to him. He spoke to me about it:

For years I knew intellectually with my mind that God loves me and all men, but for some reason it didn't do anything to me, nothing happened in me or to me; it just didn't make any difference. But in this study group, as I came into close contact with other persons who knew this forgiving love of Christ personally, it began to rub off on me until I caught it too!

This man *heard* the word of forgiveness in the forgiving fellowship; he *saw* the forgiveness of Christ in his Christian brothers and sisters. He became aware of forgiveness as he met the living Christ where two or three were gathered together in His name.

But how can *we* become aware of Christ's forgiveness? Is there any normative path marked out? Are there any constant factors which may be discerned? No blueprint can be devised to demonstrate the forgiving Christ; nor can a precise theological construction of the forgiving encounter lead us into the personal awareness. But we can be helped by observing the living, moving picture of such an encounter experienced by another person. Let me tell you of a woman who became aware of Christ's forgiveness. In her story we can find signposts and markers to guide us in our own pilgrimage. Her parents were not religious, never attended church, and were divorced when she was six years old. This was a devastating blow to her because neither parent wanted her. She writes,

I lived in five different homes over a period of several years, always feeling like an outsider looking in on other people who belonged to each other. I belonged to no one and felt alone in the world. I prided myself on never allowing myself to become vulnerable to anyone. On the whole, people had been unloving to me, and I never intended to open myself to another person for fear of getting hurt again. I didn't need anyone, and obviously no one needed me. I became hard and unsympathetic and had little understanding or concern for others and their difficulties.

Many people feel like outsiders and withdraw into a shell to protect themselves against a cruel, indifferent world. In the process they become hardened, closed in, and permanently lonely. Who is there who does not know what it means to be "unable on one's own to forgive others" or to feel "guilty and unloved oneself?"

I'm amazed now in looking back, that just at the time I was in greatest need, help came. Just when life looked hopeless, life itself was opened to me. I was extremely unhappy at this time, unhappy in my own inner life, unhappy in my marriage. I knew that I, myself, was to blame but had nowhere to turn for help. So when I went to church on Easter Sunday and heard "The Incredible Good News" [the sermon title based on the text "He appeared also to me"—I Cor. 15:8] of Christ's forgiveness, I could hardly believe my ears. My early childhood experiences made it easy for me to see myself as a sinful person —but forgiveness? *This* was something different. In prayer I had confessed my sins repeatedly but had little thought of asking for or receiving forgiveness. This is why I was so stricken when I heard that Christ loved *me* and died for *my* sins. Perhaps I had come to hate myself and to sink deeper and deeper into self-pity, knowing it was deadly but I was powerless to help myself. So indeed it was incredible good news that someone really loved me for no apparent reason, and asked only that I share with Him all that troubled me and ask Him for help and serve Him. As Olive Wyon has reminded us, "And the desert shall bloom as a rose." This is exactly what happened to me. All the time and effort I had previously put into destructive thinking was, from that time forth, spent in reading and seeking and learning about God's great love for us, for *me*, if you will.

She heard the word of forgiveness in a sermon in the midst of worship. Somehow she felt personally addressed and involved in Paul's description of his encounter with the risen Christ ("He appeared also to me"—I Cor. 15:8). The forgiveness of God became contemporary and personal in the hearing of the good news of Christ. The potential significance of the sermon is here underlined, as is the imperative to preach the grace of Christ, Christ crucified and risen for all men, for *us*! It is not coincidence that Paul preached Christ and Him crucified, or that the sermons reported in Acts stress witness to the resurrection. The word of God's grace comes to focus in the event of the cross. Preaching which penetrates to the person in his aloneness will be preaching which is addressed to the person in unfettered expectation that God can speak to him a liberating word—a word that he can truly hear and find personally liberating. There will be an urgency born of confidence in the Holy Spirit.

Aware of God's forgiving love in Jesus Christ, this woman found hope and entered upon a pilgrimage of faith, a dialogue with God in which she became increasingly aware both of her unworthiness and of Christ's mercy. The following notation is taken from a diary of her personal prayer:

I am becoming more and more aware of my ugly sinful self. It would be easier not to have faith in God than to believe that God can forgive my sins. As each new sin is forgiven and forgotten, another one rises up to take its place. . . . No deep sincere prayer for weeks. I seem enfolded and engulfed in my own self again. All I see is Jane, Jane, Jane, and I am sick to death of her. How can I do anything about it? I see the trouble; I know what is wrong, but I cannot correct it. Where do I go from here? On my knees, you say. But for some reason I am unable to do it. I can't confess my sins again. They are the same ones I have asked forgiveness for before. I'm ashamed to repeat them again!

1. The desire to be alone. Unresponsive, uncooperative, untouchable. Why?
2. Laziness.
3. Thoughtlessness of others. No letters to in-laws or friends.
4. No patience with children. Ann needs me, I know, but I can't seem to help her.

Several pages later in her diary is the following entry:

Oh such supreme joy, such relief, such happiness. Why didn't I realize it before; I can just confess my sins in one whisper to God.

I don't need to go over and over them almost enjoying the thought of how sinful I am. How foolish! The real secret is, remember Christ. He died for my sins. Remember? Just keep the cross before me. O God, thou hast taken my burden from me again, and yet again. O let me remember in times of darkness that thou art *ever* present. . . . Buttrick's book, *Prayer*, has been very important to me in these weeks of trouble, and also the prayer group has held me and kept me from falling away altogether. . . . But I've *returned!* Such joy! Such sweet lightness. Unless I had been heavy with fear and doubt I could not have known the lightness of Christ's love. O Christ, remove the accumulated trash and clutter from my life. That which does not have its beginnings in Thee must be cut out, destroyed. Strip, peel away, burn off the crust of worldliness; touch, heal, and pour over me Your gracious forgiving love.

Here is a picture of a person not progressing toward perfection but on a pilgrimage of penitence and peace. For our growth in Christ is not a matter of getting better and better, but rather a growing awareness both of guilt and grace, as the hymn verse has it—"Two wonders I confess, the wonders of redeeming love and my unworthiness."[2] Genuine progress in the Christian way consists in the deepening apprehension both of our unworthiness and of His redeeming love.

This woman remembered Christ and pondered His cross. It is when we look at Him and away from ourselves, when we consider Him and expose ourselves to Him, that healing and power come. It is the knowledge that He is with us, even in the darkness when we do not *feel* His presence, that keeps us steady. It is the study of the Word, the reading of useful books, the strength of Christian friendship, and, above all, prayer that sustains us. And let us not be suspicious of the joy of deliverance expressed in this diary. As we are delivered ourselves, we begin to understand this exuberance—and what might have seemed even extravagance—in such a hymn as Charles Wesley's "O for a Thousand Tongues to Sing," or Paul's exultant cry, "Who will deliver me from this body of death? Thanks be to God through Jesus Christ our Lord!" (Rom. 7:24, 25). Let us also take note that deliverance is not a permanent possession, but that, like this woman, we must engage ourselves in continuing penitence in the course of which new grace may pour forth.

Inevitably, the awareness of forgiveness opened the woman's life to the grace of Christ and changes began to take place in her relationships with others, and in her self-awareness.

Before coming to the church my husband and I were near the separation point. I was and still am the one who is unable fully and deeply to express my love and concern for those dearest to me. I know now this is a result of the lack of a normal loving family during my childhood. Everyone has advice, but my real need was for understanding. I was smart enough to know something was wrong; however, I was pretty sure it wasn't I. It was at this time that I came into a *koinonia* group. It's impossible fully to describe the changes that began to take place in me through the fellowship of that group. As I came to experience the love of Christ with these new friends I knew that such a love must be possible between a husband and wife. I can no longer willingly accept anything less than this forgiving and redeeming love in my marriage. I feel the responsibility is mine to create and maintain a home filled with love and a willingness to accept each other as we are.

Many couples find a new quality of relationship in a *koinonia* group. They discover a sensitivity to the feelings and attitudes of others that influences their own marriage. They begin to share ideas and hopes never discussed before and surprise each other with unsuspected depths of feeling. So this woman began to reach out to her husband, seeking deeper communication and more understanding. About a year after the previous entry, she wrote,

There was much dissension and competition between the two of us, the unco-operative you-go-your-way-I'll-go-mine type of thing. Both of us were sensitive, but neither was willing to take the risk of getting hurt or of being ridiculed. Neither of us really wanted it this way, fortunately, and I knew others had found in marriage what both of us were seeking—that is, acceptance of what we are: full, deep love for each other, and real companionship. It took me a long, long time to realize that the place to begin was with myself. And when I began to see that I must take the risk of being hurt—I must break down the barriers I had erected around myself first—then things began to happen. Little things had barred the flow of love and affection between us; now little things have happened to hasten the expressions of love we do have for each other. I see now that "loving God and ignoring husband" is impossible. If a woman is to help her husband seek to understand God's love she must express to him the same love she knows in Christ. Perhaps her husband's concept of love is determined by the love or lack of it that she expresses to him. She must approach him in humility and compassion, perhaps to be laughed at or scorned or ignored. If so, her love must be enlarged by prayer to accept this and return with a greater urgency, and fierce desire to penetrate the outer armor, believing and praying "Christ died for you and me."

The awareness of Christ's forgiveness for her opened her eyes to the truth that His forgiveness, when it comes, comes to us in our concrete relationships with others. She could only fully receive Christ's forgiveness in a forgiven and forgiving relationship with her husband. Her realization that she was called to become an agent of reconciliation in her own home is one mark of the validity of her awareness of forgiveness. As she was ministered to in the fellowship of others, she became a minister in her home, and in many other relationships. She began to be glad to be a woman!

I have a deepening sense of identification with and understanding of other women. It surprises and amazes me that I should feel really "called" to serve other women, as my relationship in the past with women was usually one of dislike and irritation at their "obvious" faults. I'm beginning to understand now that their problems are mine and their needs my own. I have discovered, much to my amazement, that we have the precious role of servant and sustainer in this life, and the fulfillment is found in entering gladly upon this work of family and home.

The opportunities for her reconciling ministry began to expand. A woman who was in the same Bible Study Group found her marriage running into serious trouble. After counseling her myself for some time, I suggested that she talk to Jane. Because the two had become dear friends, the woman felt she could share her trouble with her and did so. Thus began a healing relationship of conversation, prayer, and fellowship over a period of many months, during which time the woman's marriage was healed. Jane helped her in a way I could not possibly have done, because she had known this same pain in her own experience. Having herself been delivered, she could speak with power and conviction to one in a similar situation. When this woman and her family moved away from the community and church, she told me that her releasing friendship with Jane had saved her marriage.

In the years that followed, Jane ministered with rare compassion to numbers of people. Because she had suffered much herself, she was able to help others in their loneliness and despair and share with them for forgiving acceptance of Christ. In time her ministries extended to people in the inner city of Cleveland, and all the while she was living in an unfolding new world in which God's glory was shining. She wrote again in her diary:

At the beginning of my pilgrimage I was in desperate need, confused, and unhappy. I needed You and You poured forth Your healing power in great quantities. Whenever I stumbled and fell, You lifted me tenderly and comforted me. You were always there within sound of my voice. I feel now, however, a partner, not a wretched beggar always hungry, but now at times filled and full, strong and whole. . . . I awoke Sunday morning early, before the rest of the family, looked out of the bedroom window and saw the early morning sun just touching the roses in our neighbor's garden, felt real warmth from Your sun, and warm breezes thrilled my body. In church that morning surrounded by knowing smiles and winking eyes and whispered "hellos," my ears filled with joyous songs to You, my eyes darting about to see Your beloved community, my heart throbbing within at the beauty and joy cast about to all who would open themselves to You. Working in the afternoon with Bill and the children in the yard; bowing our heads together and eating heartily at supper; Bible study later with dear friends in Christ; the overpowering glory of Your night. You paraded all these gifts before my eyes. Before, without You, I was nothing but thought I could get along. Now I see that the words "without You" are suggestive of an impossible situation. I may withhold myself from You, deny Your existence, reject and refuse Your gifts; but the gifts are still given, and Your seeking, caring, forgiving love is ever present, ever open to me.

We are called into the church to accept Christ's forgiveness. We are sent into the world to share Christ's reconciliation. Awareness of forgiveness in the church enables us to become agents of reconciliation in the world.

Chapter 7

Agents of Reconciliation

*All this is God's doing for He has reconciled
us to Himself through Jesus Christ, and He has
made us agents of the reconciliation.*
II Corinthians 5:18, Phillips

In my study is a small window which has a screen in front of it. Every morning when I go into the study I swing back the screen and look out at the sky and trees. Through the screen everything has the pattern of the screen upon it: things are gray, colorless, blurred. But when the screen is removed the world becomes clear and distinct, and I can see things as they really are.

When Christ forgives us, the screen of illusion is taken away from our eyes, and we look out upon a new world, able now to discern ourselves and others with a new honesty. It has happened to me in this way. As the screen is removed and then removed again and again, I see myself each time more clearly and truly. And what I see is not pleasant. I become aware of myself as a guilty person. Yet what enables me to see my guilt is the presence of grace. In the light of grace I can begin to see the darkness of my sin. As my awareness of guilt grows in the presence of grace, I find myself looking upon my brother with new eyes and see something in his eyes I did not see before, and feel a compassion for him which is new.

Awareness of guilt, grace, and compassion—all three—seems to dawn afresh upon me. I cannot say which of the three comes to my consciousness first. But I know that I am most surprised and appalled at the vision of myself as I really am, or at least as I am given to see myself. I see that I am subject to moods of depression and despair, and again to flights of unbounded pride. I look into myself and see all the cardinal sins there; and I sense how tenuous is my hold on respectability, how narrow is the edge along which I have blithely and blindly been walking—nay, even presuming to lead others! As Robert Louis Stevenson puts it in one of his beautiful prayers, I remember "the horror of misconduct, from which [my] feet have been plucked out of dishonor . . . [my] sins forgiven or prevented, [my] shame unpublished."[1] I wonder how it is that God has brought forth any good purpose out of me.

At the same time that I sense my own unworthiness, I am aware of the incredible love of God, for *me*! How can it be? From my own depths I can see more clearly the heights of God's love, the love which brings Him down to me, not to condemn but to save. With the lifting power of His love I look out and really see my brother and discern a worth in him I had not noticed before. Grace shows me my unworthiness, and the worth of my brother. Awareness of Christ's forgiveness for me draws me close to my brother, and I begin to understand that whatever separates us is as nothing to that which unites us—our common need of forgiveness. The forgiveness of Christ gives me new eyes, a new outlook. "From now on, therefore, we regard no one from a human point of view" (II Cor. 5:16).

There is a new point of view that radically alters my understanding of others. I find that I am less concerned with judging another, and more concerned to go and stand with him. As I become aware of the strange "Jekyll-Hyde" character of my own being, I become more tender toward my fellow sinner. For I understand that, as I have previously overestimated my own capacity for goodness, I have underestimated his. As I become aware of alien powers of evil within me, I wonder what demonic forces may be driving my brother. If I have misunderstood myself, I have misunderstood him. If I am a paradox of good and evil to myself, he is an even greater mystery to me, and it is no longer possible to label him. There is a complexity in my brother that is marvelous and defies analysis.

J. W. Stevenson speaks of a man who is like us:

Within the same man, this tenderness and this hardness, this agony of concern and this indifference. . . . it was . . . a cleavage between his pity and his profits. He was still wanting to do opposite things with his life. The same impulse from God was obeyed or driven out of reckoning. And John Sanderson was not alone in it. This was not just inconsistency within human nature. It was something which split human nature in two; it had its origins far back in human life. Something had been set in the heart of man which made him capable of thinking more of the good of others than of his own, and of laying down his life for people he did not know; and something else within him kept telling him not to be a fool, to get out of life what he could for himself. Whatever we believed about ourselves, this could not be denied; we were selfish; we were willing to sacrifice.[2]

There is a wonder and a humiliation in this. I wish I could erase all my spoken and thought condemnations of others, retroactively. I have so much now to accomplish in the attempt to extract the beam from my own eye, and I feel ridiculous and ashamed that I have presumed to judge another. I am willing now to accept the criticism of another, because I begin to understand that only as I face myself as I am and accept the forgiveness of my brother and repent before God will I be truly free. I, who have been correcting, need correction. I, who have been leading, need to be led. Now I begin to understand why Jesus warned men continually not to judge, not to condemn, and not to think one is better than another. For it is precisely this attitude of condemnation that separates me from my brother and him from me. "If all men are afraid of each other, pupils of teachers, teachers of pupils, husbands of wives, wives of husbands, ministers or priests of their parishioners, and parishioners of their spiritual leaders, it is because all are afraid of being judged."[3]

This is why the forgiveness of Christ makes all the difference! If, in Christ, God takes me in my very unworthiness and holds me and does not leave me, and indeed offers me a way out of my guilt, I am literally rescued from myself. If God does not condemn me, He who knows me utterly, who am I to condemn myself? If He has shown His steadfast love for me by coming to me even in the midst of my unworthiness, I can for the first time face my unworthiness and accept the truth about myself, because He believes in me and cares about me and confers worth upon me. His forgiving grace opens the possibility of reconciliation with my brother. Grace is the common and holy ground upon which we can both stand and discover ourselves to be brothers. In the presence of grace I find that I can love a man with whom I violently disagree.

But we are not so easily reconciled. For the natural alienation of man from man is not merely individual but collective. My brother and I are caught and bound in structures of separation. Our blinders are fashioned and held in place from birth so that our vision is distorted and perverted. *The Enemy Camp*, a novel by Jerome Weidman,[4] describes the life of a Jewish family living in a ghetto in New York City in the early years of this century. The little boy, who is the chief figure of the novel, grew up in fear and ignorance and suspicion of all people who were not Jews. Gentiles were, to him, the enemy camp—those who were different, somehow opposed to him, the other side, those who threatened his security. A bar across the street from his room and frequented by Gentiles was for him the outpost of the enemy camp.

We have all grown up in some sort of ghetto, privileged or underprivileged, knowing only our own kind and taught to view other groups as the enemy camp. Forsaking mankind, we cling to "our kind." We learn to fear some groups and to have contempt for others. We huddle together with those who are like us. Our great yearning to belong, to be accepted by those whom we regard as our peers or whose peers we wish to become, drives us into special associations in clubs and organizations. The membership of such groups is exclusive, and the very exclusiveness is calculated to increase our security because we belong. But we discover that we have to draw the circle ever more narrowly in order to maintain security against the encroachment of others. Even inside our clubs and in-groups there are smaller and more exclusive cliques, and we look enviously at them and calculate how to be included. The principle of our own longed-for security becomes of necessity the exclusion of others. As the circle is drawn tighter, we assign more and more people to the enemy camp. Structures of separation where we live, work, and play are the context of our alienation. This is the human condition in which we all abide; this is the human point of view.

But the Christian no longer regards other men from the human point of view! The Christian has a new outlook; his eyes have been converted; he begins to see other persons with the eyes of Christ. He looks over at the enemy camp and begins to discern brothers and sisters. He can no longer measure another by the external signs of race, culture, occupation, bank account, politics, or nationality but seeks to perceive the inner person. All the false psychological and social barriers melt away under the heat of God's grace. In the light of grace he perceives personal worth and significance in the people of the enemy camp.

A friend of mine who was a teacher in a suburban school in Cleveland went on to teach in an urban college. There he found a fascinating diversity of students.

Recently, I observed a class of ninth-graders; more than half of them are over seventeen years old, all born in Puerto Rico; none read over fifth-grade level. The student teacher was doing an excellent job, and so were the students at their level. On the same day and in the same school I saw a "special progress" class that was better informed as a group than any class I had in Cleveland. In this class were many of Puerto Rican background plus Negroes and whites (East European and Italian background), all living in below average housing areas. In my own classes in the college— both graduate and undergraduate—I have Negro and white, primarily Jewish and Catholic, with some Protestants and some "nothing."

This year, for the first time in my life, I have come to the full realization that persons I believed to be radically different from myself are in fact real persons full of the emotions and rational activities that white Protestant suburbanites have. Color and creed soon recede into the background and personhood comes to the forefront. Here is someone beautiful, there is someone hurt. And pretty soon one realizes that all around are persons like oneself who want to be regarded as selves in their own right and not as members of a group.

Beneath the cross we hear the word, "Father, forgive them; for they know not what they do" (Luke 23:34). We know that this word is addressed to us and to our separated brothers. Awareness of forgiveness enables us to become agents of reconciliation, called to work actively for the reunion of those who are separated, called to abolish the enemy camps, to tear down the walls of alienation.

Here is an astounding ethic! It is not the ethic of accepting things as they are, or of letting nature take its course. It is the ethic of active involvement in bringing the separated together. If forgiveness is the great word of the Gospels, reconciliation is the great word of the Letters of the New Testament to describe the nature and purpose of the Christian life. We are sent into the world of family, work, and community to be agents of reconciliation.

In the previous chapter we saw a woman becoming an agent of reconciliation in her marriage. Tensions are often high in family relationships. Admiration and contempt alternate, gratitude and resentment jostle each other, and love and conflict abide together. The family is the primary community in which every person is called to a reconciling ministry.

But the context of daily work is set in structures of separation which can be equally impervious and unyielding. The enemy camp is always there in the shape of union or management, customer or salesman, boss or subordinate. Status and rank within the corporate structure and personality conflicts add to the tension. All of these structured hostilities are exacerbated by the necessity of earning a living in the midst of it all. How can a man be an agent of reconciliation in his job?

I have a friend who is the supervisor of a laboratory in a chemical plant. One evening in conversation he mentioned his worry about problems at work. He told me that there was a climate of backbiting and antagonism throughout the plant, then spoke of the hostile relationship between himself and one of the men whose work he supervised. This man had been doing poor work for the last five years. Several times over the years my friend had made direct efforts to communicate helpfully with him and to remedy the situation. All efforts had failed, and a silent, hostile impasse had developed between them. And all the while the work continued to be done poorly. I asked my friend, "Did you ever pray for this fellow?" A stunned look came over his face, almost as though I had struck him. He replied that he had never prayed for the man. Our conversation turned to other matters.

Two weeks later I received an excited call from him, telling me that he had achieved a breakthrough with his estranged co-worker. The night of our conversation and for several days thereafter he had prayed for the man, asking God's guidance in their relationship. In the course of prayer and meditation he came to the decision to speak to the man again, but this time on the basis of Christian concern. In order to clarify his thoughts he wrote out the things he wanted to say, and showed the statement to his wife for her comment. She suggested that he give the written statement to the man instead of speaking to him, so that he could read it and react to it in private. So the statement was re-written with that in mind. At nine-thirty the next morning he gave the statement to his co-worker, with the suggestion that later in the day they might discuss its contents. A portion of the statement follows:

A recent circumstance in my life in church has caused me to re-examine my relationship not only to God, but to my family, my friends, my associates at work, and the company I work for. . . .

In this re-examination I have thought long and hard and prayed on the particular relationship between you and me. . . . Our relationship, in my mind, had deteriorated because I was willing to let a situation persist with which I was unhappy, but one, nevertheless, about which I felt powerless to do anything. My new state of mind will no longer let me do this. . . . Thus for several days I have searched my soul to determine whether there is a basis for my feeling that you are giving only half or thereabouts of yourself to your job. . . . I might add that I would not labor over this problem, a problem that has bothered me to an unbelievable extent, if I didn't have regard for you as a man and for your family.

The statement then specifically defined the deficiencies in the man's work and ended with the hope that there could be open and honest conversation about the matter.

At about eleven-thirty that morning the co-worker handed the supervisor a written statement of his own. It began,

To cause you mental anguish is something I would not want to do. That I have caused it I do not doubt, knowing your sincerity, humanity, and kindness of nature. Many factors have been responsible for an indolent demeanor on my part. It serves no purpose to discuss them. It is sufficient that I am cognizant of them and will put them aside.

The note went on to inquire about the "new state of mind" which had caused the supervisor to act in this fashion. The two men agreed to meet together over the lunch hour the next day to discuss the whole situation.

A remarkable change was occurring in the relationship of these two men. Where there had been closed minds and resentful hearts, there was now the possibility of a new coming together. What cracked the barrier separating them was one man's courage to approach another man on a genuinely personal basis. When they met together the next day, they both felt gratitude and excitement in the realization that they were being reconciled, and that God was in it! They expressed their resentments and their new hopes freely and discussed all aspects of their personal and work relationships. Each man affirmed his desire and intention to rectify attitudes and procedures which had created their previous hostility. They decided to meet together once a week for several weeks to continue the discussion of their own relationship and to consider how they might, together, work to bring about a climate of reconciliation in the laboratory and entire plant. The co-worker said, "This is the first time I have consciously brought my religion into my work." This first luncheon meeting was concluded with a prayer by the supervisor.

The two men met together once a week for lunch for seven weeks. Significantly, the supervisor left the executive dining room, in which he was entitled to eat, to have a home-packed lunch with the other man in his office. On each occasion they shared a few moments of silence, a reading of Scripture or some pertinent article, discussion, and prayer. As their own new relationship was consolidated, they discussed possible ways of reaching out to others in the plant with their new-found spirit of reconciliation. Finally, they decided to invite several men to participate in a weekly luncheon group for the express purpose of fostering better relationships among men in the various departments of the plant. With great care and judicious planning they considered which men to ask, seeking to include men of different departments and varying job responsibilities. Eight men were approached, and all agreed to come to a meeting to hear about the proposed experiment.

My friend prepared carefully for the first meeting. He read every book and magazine article we could find that dealt with group discussions similar to those he planned. He prayed over a period of many days for every man coming to the meeting. When the men gathered for that first meeting, he read them an opening statement setting forth the proposed experiment of nine luncheon meetings. The purpose of meeting together would be to get to know one another personally, and together to explore God's will for relationships in the plant. The hope was that all might grow in understanding the nature of their responsibilities to one another and to the company. He expressed the faith that significant things might well happen as a result of their being together in this way. As a meeting pattern for lunch he suggested informal conversation, a reading on some aspect of work and society, silence, sharing of ideas and experience, and a prayer in conclusion. Finally, he suggested that, if the experiment were fruitful, other men in the plant be invited to participate.[5]

The experiment was highly successful. The sharing of personal autobiography in the meetings rapidly revealed these men to one another in an utterly new light. One said, "I have worked in this plant for over twenty-five years but I learned things about some of you fellows in the last nine weeks that I never knew before." Attendance was nearly 100 per cent for all meetings. A freedom of discussion emerged in which it was possible to air grievances and hostilities without cutting the lines of communication. It was unanimously decided to continue the group when the nine-week experiment concluded, and to form another group for others in the plant who had shown interest.

One Manday noon I shared lunch and discussion with one of these groups. Eight men were present: some Protestants, a Roman Catholic, others not affiliated with any church. Only three were actively involved in the life of a church. Their clothing varied from overalls to shirt and tie; their job responsibilities covered the range of the work in the plant. That day they were discussing selected paragraphs of *God and the Day's Work.*[6] Their conversation was open and free; they were together as friends in the midst of structures which had separated them. I felt the presence of God in that hour more surely than I have in many services of worship. Here was a tiny but infinitely significant outpost of the church in the world of work.

No one can foretell what the future holds for these groups of men seeking to participate creatively and harmoniously in productive work together. There is a new Spirit at work in that plant, a holy and reconciling Spirit. And this came to pass because one man, moved by the Spirit, was willing to become an agent of reconciliation in his place of work. I have given his experience in detail in the hope that men and women who read it will find courage and guidance to exercise a reconciling ministry in their own spheres of work. Such a ministry will, of course, take different shape in different work circumstances. It is not my intention to suggest a blueprint for reconciliation in plants or factories, but to give a concrete example of it. Each reader will apply the experience to his own situation.

It struck me that the closed mind and heart of the co-worker were penetrated because he was approached unashamedly on a spiritual basis. That his supervisor should consider him primarily as a person and not in his occupational role, and should care enough about him to pray for him—this was what reached him. It takes faith in God to pray for a fellow worker from whom one is estranged; it takes personal courage to acknowledge to him that one regards him in this perspective. The willingness to affirm openly, in appropriate fashion, that one believes in the efficacy of prayer in such a situation can change that situation utterly.

I am impressed to note several instances of this personal approach in the studies of Paul Tournier, a Christian psychiatrist. In fact, for one seeking to understand what it means to be an agent of reconciliation in his job, I can think of no better beginning than to read Tournier's *The Meaning of Persons*. Here is a living portrait of a man seeking to be used redemptively by God in the sphere of his daily work. Tournier writes,

A man may spend years in an office, seeing in his employees only their work, their good qualities and their failings, and then, when personal contact is established, suddenly discover what lies behind the façade: the secret sufferings, the sequels of unhappy childhood, disappointed hopes, struggles to remain faithful to ideals. Then too he may understand the profound significance of the qualities and failings he has seen, and the meaning that work can have when it is no longer a thing but the activity of a community of persons. . . . In the world of persons all one's professional relationships take on a new character. They become shot through with a joy that was absent when they were merely the fulfilling of a function. Everything becomes an occasion for personal contact, a chance to understand others and the personal factors which underlie their behaviour, their reactions and opinions. It is much more interesting, as well as important, to understand why some one has a certain failing, than to be irritated by it; to understand why he maintains a certain point of view than to combat it; to listen to confidences than to judge by appearances. . . . The atmosphere of office, workshop or laboratory is rapidly transformed when personal fellowship is established between those who previously criticized or ignored each other.[7]

Dr. Tournier speaks of "the medicine of the person" as that approach of the doctor to the patient which goes beyond the doctor's technical competence to the personal concern for him, in which a clinical or professionally detached relationship becomes personal. As Christians we are all called to a ministry of personal concern for those with whom we work. Such a ministry will require us to pray for our fellow workers, and in appropriate ways to become personally involved with them as agents of God's reconciling purpose in our place of work.

If we can seek to be agents of reconciliation in family life and on the job, it is more difficult to know how we can become effective reconcilers in the larger community of city and nation and world. Responsible participation in community organizations which serve a useful purpose is a clear imperative. Responsible involvement in politics and the informed exercise of the vote are equally clear imperatives. Perhaps we can clarify our responsibility in the public realm by recognizing the deepest structures of separation which prevail in our society—the separations of race, religion, nationality, and culture. These prejudices are sometimes recognized objectively and renounced in our thoughts and words but are often embedded in the structures of our actual existence.

An example of this built-in prejudice is afforded by the fashionable community of Grosse Point, Michigan, a suburb of Detroit. The Grosse Point Property Owners Association conceived a plan to measure the worth and desirability of a buyer seeking a home in that community. A point system was used to grade a prospective purchaser on the basis of race, religion, nationality, accustomed dress, accent in speaking, supposed income, appearance, etc. Passing grades were based on a sliding scale of one hundred points. Anglo-Saxons of high income could pass with relatively low scores. Poles could pass with a score of fifty-five, southern Europeans with seventy-five, Jews with eighty-five. Negroes and Orientals were automatically disqualified. A corporation representative said that a person with a very swarthy complexion would probably get a low rating.

This kind of prejudice is usually implemented by "gentlemen's agreements" in large numbers of urban and suburban neighborhoods in this country. It is precisely the same principle or philosophy of exclusion by external measurements that underlies the policy of *apartheid* in South Africa and provided the rationale for Hitler's "total solution" of the Jewish problem in the Second World War. The stupidity of this system of personal appraisal is seen in the fact that some of Detroit's wealthy gangsters live in Grosse Point.

The same prejudice is built into the formation and structure of most city and country clubs in America, as incisively documented in a recent book entitled *Some of My Best Friends*.[8] Readers may recall the article in *Life* Magazine about the creation of a second country club in a Midwestern city.[9] The evident reasons for the enthusiastic formation of this second club were twofold: the insecurity of the many who couldn't get into the first and most exclusive club in that city and the desire of the many to secure their own social standing, such as it was, against the encroachments of others lower on the social scale, including Negroes who were beginning to play golf on the city's public course.

In reflective moments we can see the unworthiness of motivation that characterizes most of our social discrimination. The thesis that "we want to associate with those who have something in common with us" breaks down when we exclude automatically those of a different race or religion. Culture, excellence in achievement, personal appeal, and charm are not the special prerogatives of any religion or race. But typically we shrug our shoulders, and accept things as they are, and go our way until some incident or event causes us to stop and take a second look. A personal encounter with prejudice may do it.

Some time ago I took part in a religious emphasis week at a large university. After the first evening lecture by the speaker of the week, I met with a group of freshmen in a dormitory room for discussion. We talked about the things that separate us from one another. One young man, eighteen years of age, shared with us a personal experience:

When I was ten years old I used to play with the other kids on our street. One day one of them invited me to come and swim at the country club to which his family belonged. I was excited about it and looked forward to the occasion the following week, eagerly. Then, the day before the swimming date he stopped me at school and in a strange apologetic kind of way said that he couldn't take me to the club because his parents had told him that Jews weren't welcome there. He said he was sorry.

That afternoon the ten-year-old child went home in tears, and his father tried to tell him why it is that some people don't like Jews. This was his first vivid experience of being excluded because he was a Jew. As he told us his story he stuttered. I thought to myself that his stutter could well be a result of the polite and impolite exclusion he has suffered in his life from people who call themselves Christians.

Does the inhumanity and cruelty of our gracious structures of social discrimination strike you as no longer tolerable? Is it becoming clear that there is no difference in principle between discrimination in the North and segregation in the South—only a difference in procedure? Instead of police dogs, fire hoses, and electrically charged prod poles, we Northerners use such word-weapons as "Sorry, all the rooms and cottages are rented," "Wouldn't you like to look in a neighborhood where you would feel more welcome?" "There are no more openings at present in our plant, union, apartment building, club, etc., etc." It is debat-

able which form of exclusion is more degrading. Evil in its gross
manifestations at least has an honesty about it which is denied
to those of us who hide behind turned-away faces or silent
mouths and cower on the sidelines while the battle for racial
justice continues. There is no other word for the silent Christian
in these days than hypocrite.

I have come to the conviction that I will not associate myself
as a member in any club, society, or organization that discrim-
inates in its membership and excludes others by reason of race,
religion, or any other external measurement. I acknowledge the
democratic right of freedom of association, but I assert a prior
responsibility for the Christian to repudiate structures that separate people and to identify himself with structures that seek to
reconcile people.

Most kinds of social discrimination are as foolish as assaying
the worth of a gift by its outer wrappings. It is as provincial and
obsolete as the signs in Boston a generation ago—"No Irish need
apply." How sad arbitrarily to deny oneself the stimulation and
enrichment of intimately knowing people of diverse background.
How laughable to assume that all desirable people for our neighborhood or club must live in white skins, in a world where it has
pleased God to put more than two-thirds of humanity in non-
white skins! How absurd to think that a Ralph Bunche or a
Marian Anderson or the millions of their race are not people
worth knowing. How ludicrous for a Christian to belong to an
organization in which his Lord, a Jew, would be unacceptable for
membership.

The time is past when Christians can afford the hypocrisy of
supporting social and geographical structures of separation while
acknowledging the call to be agents of reconciliation. I am convinced that a Christian involved in such a structure of separation
has two Christian alternatives. One is to remove himself from the
membership of that organization; the other is to work actively
within such a structure for elimination of the external prejudicial
barriers. The latter course may be the commitment required of

those who at present are members of discriminatory clubs or residents of discriminatory neighborhoods. We are called, as Christians, to work for and support structures of social reconciliation, and to recognize social structures of separation and discrimination as alien to the spirit and purpose of Jesus Christ.

Our prejudice at its root is not poor vision or faulty reasoning; it is unbelief. It is evidence that we still look at the world through a screen. It is disobedience and dishonesty. "If any one says, 'I love God,' and hates his brother, he is a liar" (I John 4:20). Once we reach the conclusion that Christ died for all men, we have no alternative but to accept His ministry of reconciliation in every area of our lives, with no expedient exceptions.

Perhaps the most remarkable agent of reconcilation in our time was the late Pope John XXIII. His papal encyclical "Peace on Earth" issued on Maundy Thursday, April 11, 1963, calls for a world community based on the interdependence of nations and urges men to work for the good not only of their own political and religious communities but of the entire human family. The encyclical is magnanimously addressed to "all men of good will." It is the eloquent plea of a man whose efforts were unceasingly devoted to a ministry of reconciliation. When someone asked the Pope why he decided to call an Ecumenical Council in 1962, it is said that he opened a nearby window and replied to the questioner, "To let some fresh air into the church."

As agents of reconciliation it is our task to open windows of communication and doors of fellowship where we live, work, and worship, so that the fresh air of Christ's Spirit may blow into every corner of the church and the world—that Spirit of truth which sets all men free.

Chapter 8

Freedom to Walk in the Spirit

*Christ set us free, to be free men ... If we live in
the Spirit, let us also walk in the Spirit.*

Galatians 5:1, NEB
Galatians, 5:25, AV

Once I walked into an art gallery in Florence, Italy, and my
eyes fell on a large marble sculpture. It was roughly carved and
obviously was unfinished. I drew closer to determine the subject
of the sculpture. Gradually I discerned the shapes of men locked
in struggle, with bonds of rope or iron across their straining
chests, in positions of anguished stretching, muscles bulging with
futile attempts to break loose. I remained for a moment, feeling
myself caught and bound together with those figures. The title
of this unfinished work by Michelangelo is "Slaves in Bondage."

Everyone knows something of the meaning of human bondage,
shackled as we all are to pressures outside us and within, which
stifle our liberty, muffle our communication, stultify our self-
expression, and crush our hopes. We are slaves to time and circumstance, to passions which corrupt us and ambitions which
compromise us. Margaret T. Applegarth writes that we live in
a generation of "sly, sophisticated wisecracks—all more or less
dirtbound, earthbound, skinbound, sexbound, scandalbound,

drinkbound, fashionbound, gadgetbound, noisebound. . . ."[1] You and I are there; for every man, like Marley's ghost, walks the earth to the clang of chains forged in his own life, powerless to set himself free from himself.

Paul wrote to the Galatian Christians in words which pronounced the Magna Carta of spiritual freedom for all men: "Christ set us free, to be free men. Stand firm, then, and refuse to be tied to the yoke of slavery again" (Gal. 5:1, NEB). Here is a *declaration of independence* from all human controls, from all arbitrary legalisms. Christ has set us free! Free from what? Free to be and do what?

1. *Christ frees us from the bondage of false security.* Where does your security rest? What are the props that shore up your personal confidence? What is the structure of your own inner assurance? There are various ways of finding out. Ask yourself some questions: In whose presence do I feel ill at ease—that of the boss, an important customer, someone higher than I in the social scale, someone with a lot more money or with far superior education, someone different from me in culture or color or creed? To whom do I feel superior—to what persons in my family and where I work, to what groups in my city and in the nation and world? To whom do I feel inferior? Whom do I fear and for whom do I have contempt? To whom do I look for my signals? Who are my peers? (You may have seen that cartoon in which one executive talks to another and, pointing to a third, says, "That man is vice-presidential timber. I liked the way he buttered me up!") Whom do you have to butter up, and who butters you up in family, work, and social circles?

Christ frees us from bondage of false securities because our ultimate security is in Him and in no one else. He has accepted us; therefore, it does not ultimately matter if everyone else rejects us. His judgment is the only one that finally counts. He is our Lord, and we have no other. Therefore, we need neither fear nor favor any man. "The fear of the Lord is the beginning of wisdom" (Ps. 111:10). We look to Him for our signals. We put down the pilings of our confidence deep within Him, for He gives inner assurance which the world can neither give nor take away.

2. *Christ frees us from false evaluations of personal worth.* If mercy is a thing twice blessed, then false estimates of the worth of a man are twice cursed. Cursed are those who set the standards of measurement, and cursed are those who accept such standards for themselves. I think of a fine family of modest income living in a community of great wealth where the measure of personal worth is success, defined in terms of wealth and social position. In these terms this family definitely has not made the grade. The sad fact is that the family itself accepts the community's evaluation of their personal worth, and its members suffer from a kind of hangdog shame. They cannot get into the "right" club, or any club; they can never get into the "right" social circles.

Christ delivers us from this false yardstick. When we understand that God measures our personal worth, not in terms of what we have in the bank or where we live or whom we know, but in terms of the integrity of our personal response to His love, then we are free, gloriously free to co-operate with Christ, unhindered by the gimmicks of social snobbery. If God accepts us, who are we to condemn ourselves, or to condemn another whom God has also accepted? A Christian can never forget that Jesus chose His friends not on the basis of what they could do for Him but on the basis of what He would do for them. He associated with the "wrong people" and gave His life for "the least of these."

3. *Christ frees us from a false concept of progress.* We want to feel that we are making progress, climbing ever a little higher on the ladder of life. We feel confident if we manage to get ahead in terms of material prosperity and social popularity. Consider the progress Jesus made: from poverty to nothing; from relative popularity to a criminal's death. The symbol of His "progress"

was not a promotion or a fat bonus check, but a cross. He did not make progress in the terms by which we are accustomed to evaluate our lives. He was not successful by worldly standards. Yet He made progress in terms of faithful obedience to the Father.

Christ delivers us from the slavery of feeling that we have to be making progress in worldly terms. There is a fairly successful man in Cleveland, who was offered a significant promotion that would have augmented his income considerably but would have taken him out of Cleveland to another city. He had become deeply involved in the witness of his church. After considerable thought and prayer he was convinced that it was God's will for him to continue in that particular witness. He turned down the promotion. The big thing in his life is *not* how far he can climb up the corporate ladder but where he can best serve Jesus Christ. He is a free man, free from the allurements of the world, because he has succumbed to a greater allure in Christ. He has found something, Someone, who does satisfy. The question each Christian can ask himself is, "Am I making progress on the way of the cross marked out for me?"

4. *Christ delivers us from a false longing.* Most of us find ourselves living for the future when we shall "have all the things we want" and "be able to do all the things we want." Such fruitless longing makes us discontented with our present circumstances and prevents real fulfillment in the present or the future. John Keats, observing an urn on which was painted a young man in pursuit of a maiden, pondered the fact that the joy of the chase would forever be his, and that the beauty of his beloved would never fade. He would never capture her and thus never know the sour taste of disillusionment. So Keats wrote, "for ever wilt thou love, and she be fair!"[2] Yes, but we must add, "Forever wilt thou pursue and never find; forever wilt thou long and never be fulfilled; forever wilt thou run and never rest," always living for a tomorrow that never arrives. For the world, anticipation may be

50 per cent of realization, but for the Christian there is fulfillment already in this present time because our controlling desire is only to serve Christ; and in single-minded loyalty to Him we are given a freedom to "sit loose in the saddle" to what the world calls progress, accepting both favor and scorn with equanimity.

5. *Christ delivers us from a false righteousness.* A man once said to me, "I don't swear; I don't smoke; I don't drink; I don't tell dirty stories." I felt like asking him, "Brother, what *do* you do?" Is there anything more repelling than a smug, self-righteous pharisee who neatly divides life into "dos" and "don'ts," and then separates people into sheep and goats, depending on whether they do or don't do these things? Is there anything more fatuous than to think that we can put a fence around ourselves and keep sin away from our own door? What we mean when we talk about "Christian discipline" is something far removed from the puritanical joylessness of those who would make Christianity a sternly moralistic affair.

Consider Jesus—a man to whom thieves and prostitutes and crafty merchants and rough sailors were attracted. Here was a man whom His enemies accused of being a glutton and a drunkard because He evidently enjoyed human fellowship freely and fully. Consider Him, and brush away the prudish, effeminate images you may have of Him. Begin to see Him as a real man— man at the fullest and highest expression of manhood. He was the sort of man whom religious and political authorities could regard as dangerous, a man who could start a riot in a church and increase the supply of wine at a wedding party. Throw off the petty legalisms and enter into His joy, a *joie de vivre* with that bold zest and glad daring for which we all hunger. Christ sets us free from false righteousness, preparing us for the major surrenders and the decisive prunings, the merciless cleansing which opens the way to purity and humility.

6. *Christ deliver us from a false freedom.* The man who has thrown off the bonds of legalistic moralism is tempted into an

easy acceptance of his own imperfection. To acknowledge that
one is a sinner is one thing; to shrug one's shoulders and say, "I'm
only human; I'm not a saint after all," is another. We are sinners-
called-to-be-saints and summoned to perfection. We are not free
to be content with any lesser goal. Florence Allshorn writes, "We
are suffering terribly from a kind of Christian insipidity; suffering too from a Christianity which is merely conversion, merely
service, when the goal set before us is perfection and we dare not
let any life settle on a less true foundation than that 'high calling'
of which St. Paul was so aware."[3] Christ delivers us from pseudo
freedom to a responsible liberty, drawing us out of ourselves with
transforming power to serve others.

Paul wrote to the Galatians, "You, my friends, were called to
be free men; only do not turn your freedom into license for your
lower nature, but be servants to one another in love. For the
whole law can be summed up in a single commandment: 'Love
your neighbor as yourself'" (Gal. 5:13, 14, NEB). Here is a
declaration of interdependence. We are free to become a volun-
tary slave to the neighbor. Luther puts this paradox in these
words, "A Christian man is a perfectly free lord of all, subject to
none. A Christian man is a perfectly dutiful servant of all, subject
to all."[4]

This is freedom to do what I please only as it serves my neighbor. It is freedom, not to indulge my own appetites and desires,
but to become responsibly involved in the sufferings and needs
of the neighbor.

Again Luther writes:

Although the Christian is thus free from all works, he ought in
this liberty to empty himself, to take upon himself the form of a
servant, to be made in the likeness of men, to be found in fashion
as a man, and to serve, help and in every way deal with his neighbor
as he sees that God through Christ has dealt and still deals with himself. . . . I will therefore give myself as a Christ to my neighbor,
just as Christ offered Himself to me; I will do nothing in this life
except what I see is necessary, profitable and salutary to my neighbor, since through faith I have an abundance of all good things in
Christ. Lo, thus from faith flow forth love and joy in the Lord, and

from love a joyful, willing and free mind that serves one's neighbor willingly and takes no account of gratitude or ingratitude, of praise or blame, of gain or loss. For a man does not serve that he may put men under obligations, he does not distinguish between friends and enemies, nor does he anticipate their thankfulness or unthankfulness; but most freely and most willingly he spends himself and all that he has, whether he waste all on the thankless or whether he gain a reward. . . . Hence, as our heavenly Father has in Christ freely come to our help, we also ought freely to help our neighbor through our body and its works, and each should become as it were a Christ to the other, that we may be Christs to one another and Christ may be the same in all; that is, that we may be truly Christians.[5]

The content of Christian life together is an interdependent priesthood. Each Christian is called to mediate Christ's love to the other in a mutual ministry of forgiveness and burden-bearing. The church is called to prefigure and embody the ministry of reconciliation which is God's purpose for the world.

The dynamic of Christian freedom is gratitude to God for His generous, gracious mercy toward us in Christ. Sometimes we become aware of the grace of God through the grace of a brother or a father. When my father went to college, his father gave him a checkbook with authority to write checks according to his needs. Through the college years his father added money to the account as necessary. Long after my father had graduated from college, he asked his father how much it had cost to finance his college education. His father replied, "I don't know. I didn't keep track." "But," said my father, "how did you know whether I was playing fair with you and not spending more money than I really needed?" "Oh," replied his father, "if you weren't playing fair with me, I didn't want to know it."

When we find out by surprise that someone has been loving us like that for years, in a magnanimous, trusting way, exposing himself to be abused or taken advantage of by us, we can scarcely endure it. We search for adequate ways of saying "thank you" but never find them. When we begin to understand that God has been loving us like that since the day of our first breath, that in

Christ He offered Himself to us to be ignored or ridiculed or rejected if such was to be our response, gratitude wells up in our hearts. A desire rises up within us to please God by loving His children in the same way He has loved us. That which had been grudging duty now becomes glad obedience. Yes, it is grace that touches off our gratitude and makes us want to give as freely as we have received. William Maltby gave expression to his own experience of grace in a poem called "The Manse":

> When I was a child and had nothing to pay,
> They fed me and clothed me, day upon day.
> *She* nursed me in measles and other such ills,
> And mended my clothes, and *he* paid the bills.
> They hoped for me, feared for me, prayed for me too
> And thwarted the devil and carried me through:
> And I never knew how
> And I never asked why
> They should wear out their lives for a thing such as I—
>   Well. that was their way:
> I was a child and had nothing to pay.
>
> Those days are far gone: I grew to a man,
> A respectable person, according to plan,
> Took sixteen in collars and wore a black coat,
> Political candidates called for my vote;
> I wrote to the papers and gave them my views,
> And preached to the people all patient in pews,
> I was paid once a quarter and had an account
> At the Bank, with a pass-book to show the amount.
>   Was it worth all their trouble?
> Oh! *Not all* my building was wood, hay, and stubble,
> Not all my striving was done for the hire.
> A hireling's reward——and fit for the fire.
>
> Some scruples of gold God gave to my hand,
> Some pieces of silver would fall as He planned,
> Some stones that were hewn from the quarry of old
> Blood-tinctured, enduring and fair to behold:
> But how much was there that could meet His desire?
> And how much for burning and fuel of fire?

> If He calls for a reckoning, ah! what shall I say?
> "Lord, this poor debtor has nothing to pay."
> "Nothing to pay!
> Give him justice," they say—
> "Nothing for nothing, and have him away."
> But a voice said: "Yet, stay!
> Grace is for those who have nothing to pay."
> Well! that is His way:
> Grace is for those who have nothing to pay.[6]

In the presence of grace we discover our spiritual bankruptcy. In the freedom of grace we know our bondage. Our very freedom is a gift. Here is a *declaration of dependence* on God's grace, for we who cannot do the good we want to do are also those who do the evil we want to avoid. We are engaged in a struggle between the Spirit of God in us and what Paul calls our "lower nature" (Gal. 5:16, NEB). Only as our false self is shed can our true self be released to life. As each layer of falsity falls away from us, we become more real and free. But it is a constant and never ending struggle. Jacques Ellul writes,

> . . . the Christian life is always an "agony," that is, a final decisive conflict: thus it means that constant and actual presence in our hearts of the two elements of judgment and grace. But it is this very fact which ensures our liberty. We are free, because at every moment in our lives we are both judged and pardoned, and are consequently placed in a new situation, free from fatalism, and from the bondage of sinful habit.[7]

How difficult it is for us to believe that at every moment God judges and pardons us, and thus that we are really free. We fear that our guilt turns away God's grace. Such doubt dissipates our freedom. Some time ago I was experiencing a time of doubting the grace of God. A general and heavy sense of unworthiness weighted upon me. I tried to pray about it and confessed those things I knew to confess. But I did not trust the sincerity of my own prayers and felt further guilt in wondering whether I really was repenting of my sins. And then one day I was outside, reading. The sun began to rise above the trees, and I became conscious of its warmth on my arms and forehead. Suddenly there came into my mind the words of Jesus about the heavenly Father who "makes his sun rise on good and bad alike, and sends the rain on the honest and the dishonest" (Matt. 5:45, NEB). Hallelujah! The sun was shining on me, even me! My guilt had *not* turned away His grace. I felt an inrush of free joy in the assurance of full acceptance by God. Once again the doors of life swung open and the winds of heaven were blowing on me. Christ sets us free to live in the Spirit, to breathe the fresh air of heaven's freedom on earth. The Spirit is the *élan vital* of God, the power moving us into new Life. Paul writes, "If we live in the Spirit, let us also walk in the Spirit" (Gal. 5:25, AV). What does it mean to walk in the Spirit?

To walk in the Spirit means to walk in the creativity of faith. We lose faith so quickly—faith in God, faith in one another, faith in ourselves. We become disillusioned or hurt and begin to doubt and drift. We put a ceiling on our expectations and settle into the rigid confines of an existence that has stalled on dead center. The Holy Spirit restores the creativity of faith. He enables us to venture forth not knowing where we are going or what is ahead, with the confidence to trust God in the dark, and with courage to do an utterly new thing.

Florence Allshorn was this sort of creative person. A friend said of her, "She gave me the impression of toughness and delicacy, like silver wire." After several years spent in Africa as a missionary, working in the midst of overwhelming difficulties with quiet and cheerful endurance, she returned to England to form a training center for missionaries, St. Julian's Community, known as one of the lighthouses of faith in the Christian world today. Florence Allshorn wrote,

I think my sin is aimlessness, but it's difficult to know what to aim at. I do want to justify my existence. There's such a zest in life just now. I feel life's just starting again. I believe I shall all my life be chucking up the old things and going in for new, because it's so invigorating pelting into the unknown, and I believe I shall always be falling out of the frying pan into the fire. And God save me from ever settling down. . . . These are the things that daunt you—the shallows of yourself. Still I'm not going to be daunted. I'm out for the hazard again. Is it so impossible to live up to your utmost? I'll dare to try.[8]

Rushing into the unknown, daring to try—this is the creativity of faith that gives us the courage to fail, to risk defeat for a great victory. Is this faith obsolete in a disillusioned and cynical generation? John Ciardi, writing of the security-minded youth of our day, says, "They are so afraid of going broke that they are unwilling to go for broke."[9] If Ciardi is right, it is a sad thing, for all major creative achievements in life come from a faith that is willing to go for broke.

I see this kind of courage as often in older people as in youth. For what I speak of is not brash overconfidence but courageous trust born of suffering and undergoing without going under. Reuel Howe dedicated his book *The Creative Years*[10] in this fashion: "To My Mother who is in her eighty-first creative year." Creativity has to do, not with age, but with the Spirit, who inspires the artist, drives the writer, and haunts the inventor. This is the Spirit who releases the creative energies in you and in me. For we all have resources of which we are scarcely aware. Beneath the ordinary personage is the extraordinary person waiting to be released.

Creativity is the rare combination of imagination and daring, sensitivity and courage. The Spirit frees us to be open to all experience and to be alert to that which is significant in people and events. We are enabled to accept a new approach without making it a fad, and to let it go when it has lost its value. We are free to grow and change and learn. E. Herman describes this creative freedom:

And if a will of iron represents one aspect of the liberated soul, flexibility and detachment of spirit represent a complementary aspect. To obey the inspirations of grace moment by moment, to adjust oneself readily to the promptings of a living Master, is a task which demands the glorious liberty that is the high prerogative of the sons of God. Complete docility to the Divine Guide, instant response to His most fragmentary suggestions, and unhesitating readiness to go where He sends us, even though the call of today seems to contradict the command of yesterday—such flexibility presupposes a royal heart of devotion which defies human canons of consistency and looks to God only.[11]

To walk in the Spirit means to walk in the certainty of hope. We easily lose hope in family and work relationships. Attitudes become rigid and expectations fixed. We accept things as they are and will not believe that they can be changed. We slip into despair. Someone has said that despair is peculiarly a Christian sin because the Christian has a vision of what might be. His despair is the realization of how far short he falls. The Holy Spirit renews the certainty of hope, a hope that does not disappoint us because it is based on God's decisive action in Christ. When Paul writes, "For we have been saved, though only in hope" (Rom. 8:24, NEB), he means that the crucial event has taken place. We live now in the time between that saving act and its final fulfillment. We live in hope of that which we already know in part. The Spirit at work in us is pledge and guarantee that God will complete what He has begun.

To walk in the certainty of hope means to focus on God, for whom all things are possible, instead of dwelling upon our own impotence or the seeming intractability of our circumstances. We can set no limits on God's power or possibility. Florence Allshorn writes,

I think if you love God with . . . patience and passion . . . you get fundamentally out of the hands of men; they can alter your doings and beings but they can't prevent them. I mean the will of God will come through you in one way if not in another, and it's the most beautifully safe feeling.[12]

Here is the knowledge that our real security and joy are in Him who is the beginning and end of life. Here is the Spirit of hope that was also beating in the heart of that exuberant Christian

community described in the Book of Acts. Here is the Spirit
that sustains a man in time of defeat and teaches him new insights
and gives him courage. It is the hope that keeps a man from giving
up on himself or another. It is the hope that enables a husband and
wife to work through a time of danger in their marriage to a new
strength and sensitivity. It is the Spirit that ever keeps alight the
vision of what could be and refuses to accept failure and death
as the final word.

To walk in the certainty of hope is to know that nothing in all
creation can separate us from the love of God in Christ. It is
to know that we are held by a love that will not let us go. Here
is the confidence of Martin Luther, who could write:

> A mighty fortress is our God
> A bulwark never failing;
> Our helper He, amid the flood
> Of mortal ills prevailing:
>
> *
>
> Let goods and kindred go,
> This mortal life also;
> The body they may kill:
> God's truth abideth still,
> His Kingdom is forever.[18]

Here is the assurance of John Wesley who knew his sins were
forgiven. Here is the power of every Christian—the knowledge
that, in Christ, God has established his beachhead of love in the
world. Though many battles are yet to be fought, victory is
assured.

To be a Christian is to face overwhelming odds with a confidence that seems absurd to the observer. The young collegians
who began the sit-ins in the South several years ago sang spirituals
when they were arrested and taken to jail. The spiritual most
often sung ends with the chorus, "We shall overcome; we shall
overcome." And they *shall* overcome; they are overcoming, and
they know it. They ride the crest of the wave of the future,
which belongs to God, and which no man can finally deter.

To walk in the Spirit means to walk in the spontaneity of love.
That which we call love cools down, hardens into habit, settles
into fixed patterns of stimulus and reaction. The little shoots of
joy or affection are blighted by a sky that get permanently
cloudy. There are no more surprises. Paul Tournier writes,

> How many married couples no longer know how to tell each other
> quite simply that they love each other? Even joy is often smothered.
> Yesterday evening a mother announced to me the engagement of
> her daughter. "You approve of the young man?" I asked. "Oh,
> absolutely!" "Then I hope you flung your arms round her neck and
> told her so." "No, I didn't dare to. I told her it was getting late,
> and she had better go to bed, and that we should talk about it some
> other time. . . ."[14]

How sad it is when we are unable to rejoice with those who rejoice and weep with those who weep. The Holy Spirit rekindles
the spontaneity of love and frees us from crippling inhibitions to
express the love that is inside us.

A child knows this freedom to be himself and to express what
he feels. When our family returned one year from summer vacation, our eight-year-old daughter ran into our home, looked
joyously around at all the familiar sights of the house, and said
to her mother, "Oh, mommy, how do you hug a house?" How
glorious to be able to be what you are, to let the smile in your
heart show on your face. How glad to be able to express the im-
pulsive word of thanks or apology that rises to our lips, a word
which so often is stifled because of propriety or "good taste" or
shyness. It is the Holy Spirit who prompts us to make the gesture
of friendship which we feel when we feel it, to write the note
when the thought comes to mind, to make the telephone call or
personal visit. How much joy is lost to the world because we re-
press our response to the promptings of the Spirit out of fear
that it will be misunderstood or ignored!

A spontaneous gesture of love or compassion may have un-
dreamed-of effects. Paul Tournier records a conversation with a
young man who described to him the decisive moment of his
life.

Torn in early youth by the Second World War from a life of wealth and ease, and hunted by the Nazis who had invaded his country, he was destitute and in flight at the time. In the street he saw an itinerant vendor selling buns, but he had no money with which to buy any. A wretched beggar came up and bought himself one, and then, turning and seeing him standing there, offered it to him instead of eating it himself. That simple, spontaneous gesture overwhelmed the young man. It was a complete revelation to him; it made a different man of him. And ever since that day he has been tormented by the continual camouflage in which civilized society indulges. "I cannot board a trolley-bus," he told me, "without feeling an urge to offer up a   silent prayer at the sight of all those people packed together, eyeing each other, judging each other by appearances, calculating their chances and trying to keep themselves in countenance."[15]

Haven't you felt an odd compassion on occasion for some total stranger walking along the sidewalk or riding in a subway? When people don't know you are looking at them, they relax their faces and something of the hurt and hope in them comes out to be seen, and you feel your heart reaching out in the bonds of a common humanity. A friend who is a salesman has told me that sometimes when he meets a man to do business he greets him and looks him in the face and really sees the man himself, and wants to say to him, "God bless you." The world cries out for such blessing. What marvels would be wrought in human relationships if we let the Spirit free us to bless one another with uncalculated love.

Florence Allshorn writes,

I am so troubled about not loving people enough. . . . I feel somehow as if I'm not awake yet. I feel as though there is such lots more in me that somehow hasn't got a releasing touch yet. I do want to come awake, only I don't know how. . . . I used to think that being nice to people and feeling nice was loving people. But it isn't, it isn't. Love is the most immense unselfishness and it's so big I've never touched it.[16]

There are deeps of love in all of us waiting to be touched off by the Spirit, who rekindles the spontaneity of our love. Sometimes we discover that we have stifled the extraordinary gifts of a person by typing him and dismissing him as this kind of person or that kind. When we are enabled to look with fresh eyes upon another, especially one close to us in family or work, we may be amazed to see a person we never noticed before. We can be agents of the Spirit in releasing the beauty and glory of others just by being sensitive to the real person straining to come out and be known. Christ gives us freedom to walk in the Spirit, to live on the edge of joy, to stand always at the beginning of life!

Chapter 9

The Ordered Life

*The end of all things is upon us, so you must
lead an ordered and sober life, given to prayer.*
1 Peter 4:7, NEB

One evening a woman said to some friends, "My life is
gay and filled with activity; there is plenty to do, and I think
I'm relatively happy. But I have the feeling somehow that much
of it is froth, that it is really very transient, a lot of nothing. And
I wonder sometimes if I were simply to disappear whether it
would make much of a difference."

That woman has walked along the edge of emptiness. She has
begun to wonder whether it all does amount to

> . . . sound and fury,
> Signifying nothing,[1]

and if this is what Nietzsche meant when he said that God was
dead. She suffers the experience of alienation.

Alienation is the daily bread of modern man. It is the experience of being cut off or cast adrift.

. . . alienation refers to powerlessness, to the sense of being controlled by alien forces, of being unable to determine the outcome of
events: war, unemployment, race problems. Alienation refers to
meaninglessness, to the sense of being involved in complex unintel-

ligible affairs. And finally, alienation refers to what we might call self-estrangement, to the sense of being unable to realize a directly satisfying self-image, of being other-directed, of being involved in work in which intrinsic meaning has been lost in routine—being unable, that is, to participate in spontaneous acts of work and play which are their own reward.[2]

It is not my purpose or within my competence to discuss in much detail our common experience of alienation. But I may perhaps point to the particular shape it takes in our day. There is the *cosmic dimension* of alienation. In the sixteenth century, King Lear could shake his fist at the heavens and cry out.

> Blow, winds, and crack your cheeks! rage! blow!
> You cataracts and hurricanoes, spout
> Till you have drench'd our steeples. . . .
> . . . And thou, all-shaking thunder,
> Smite flat the thick rotundity o' th' world!
> Crack nature's moulds. . . .[3]

At least there was something to be cracked, something or someone to shake your fist at, some dependable order of things against which to protest. But we in the twentieth century look out into the silence of a yawning darkness, a black nothingness in which we spin on the periphery.

There is the *psychological dimension* of alienation. Modern science has long since cleared the outer world alike of angels and devils; but psychology has taken the lid off an inner world filled with devils far more terrifying than those that threatened Martin Luther. Like Narcissus we bend over, fascinated by our image in the pool of water. But what we see in our cesspool horrifies us. We do not know who we are, and what is more we are afraid to find out. We are so aware of our problems and our guilt that we doubt the goodness of our creation.

There is the *personal dimension* of alienation. We are those who suffer from the alienation of affections. We have learned how to glance off other people's lives without meeting them and knowing them. We know how to hide and dissemble and cover up. We have lost the capacity to be personal, to share ourselves. Somehow we feel unimportant, unable to have creative participation in things that matter. The individual is ineffective politically, and feels himself a cog in the industrial machine, whether on the assembly line or in the cubicle of corporate structure. In the church he finds an overweening pattern of organization which, instead of healing him and restoring his inner power, may in fact scatter his energies the more and contribute to his already considerable reservoir of unresolved guilt. This anonymity and dehumanization is most poignant in family life. T. S. Eliot gives voice to the pathos of innumerable husbands and wives in the conversation between Celia Copplestone and her psychologist.

> Oh, I thought that I was giving him so much!
> And he to me—and the giving and the taking
> Seemed so right. . . .
> And then I found we were only strangers. . . .
> Two people who know they do not understand each other,
> breeding children whom they do not understand,
> and who will never understand them.[4]

The experience of alienation finds expression in disordered, fragmented living. When we lose inner control and purpose we become subject to centrifugal pressures which misshape us. Sometimes we feel literally like the vision of ourselves in a hall of mirrors, grotesquely crushed down or pulled apart. Or we feel that we are literally "going to pieces" like the scattered bits of a jigsaw puzzle which is never put together. We never see the whole picture or discern the inner meaning. We suffer the experience of fragmentation.

Perhaps a sense of humor is the only thing that keeps us sane at times when we are almost frantic. Phyllis McGinley describes the peculiar pressures on women these days.

[Grandmother] was not expected, as we are, to combine in her one ladylike person the functions of wife, mother, interior decorator, registered nurse, child psychologist, landscape gardener, participator in public affairs, scintillating hostess, director of budgets and general good sport. She did not feel she was a failure if she could not ski, sail, keep down her weight, chair the literary section of the women's club and understand her husband's business.[5]

Sloan Wilson describes the male dilemma:

There often seems to be more desperation than contentment on the faces of men clutching the wheels of highpowered outboard motorboats, careening down icy slopes on skis or trudging up mountain trails with guns (or, we might add, glumly toting up the golf score after a fierce day of relaxation on the links). . . . husbands frequently complain that they are tired of honey-do days—days at home during which their wives keep saying, "Honey, do this and honey, do that."[6]

A sense of humor can help give us perspective but does not alter the fact that many of us are living on a carousel that goes round and round but never seems to come out here, or there, or any specific place. After a while the merriness of it all fades away and we move from boredom to resignation and the final shrug.

Aimlessness is the result of an alienated, fragmented existence. It is appropriate that the recently written creed of the United Church of Christ asks God's forgiveness for "aimlessness and sin." This lack of direction consists in a loss of urgency, the feeling that nothing significant ever happens to one. There is a marked absence of passion in the young people of our day. In a recent book entitled *Come and Join the Dance*, Joyce Glassman writes:

What if you lived your entire life completely without urgency? You went to classes, you ate your meals, on Saturday nights a boy you didn't love took you to the movies. Now and then, you actually had a conversation with some one. The rest of the time you spent waiting for something to happen to you. When you were particularly desperate you went out looking for it.[7]

Aimlessness finally resolves itself in self-pity and a loss of nerve. Nowhere does it find more graphic expression than in the most famous college song of America, "The Whiffenpoof Song":

> We are little black sheep who have lost our way, baa, baa, baa.
> We are little black sheep who have gone astray, baa, baa, baa.
> Gentlemen, songsters, off on a spree
> Damned from here to eternity.
> God have mercy on such as we,
> Baa-baa-baa.

This is a song of resignation to that which is "bigger than both of us," and a song of surrender from a world that ends

> Not with a bang but a whimper,[8]

a song that appropriately ends in plaintive bleating.

Into this uneasy mood of impending judgment in a world off on a spree comes the tolling of the bell of Scripture: "The end of all things is upon us" (I Pet. 4:7, NEB). This word of end came to the people of the first century, who thought that history was not moving. This word of the end was the declaration that *the* event of history had happened, that eternity had personally penetrated time, and that a new age was inaugurated. It was the word that God was alive and had taken decisive action on our behalf in Jesus Christ. From then on, every decision had meaning and urgency.

"The end of all things is upon us" is a word of peculiar power and relevance to us of the twentieth century. We who live under the shadow of the bomb are reminded that we always live under the shadow of the Almighty, that life is not skin deep but sky high, that the Christian always lives in the time of the end. For the Christian it is always the time of making decisions which shape his destiny, the time in which things *do* matter and there *is* ultimate meaning. We watch the breakdown of civilizations and the rise of new ones without trepidation because we know that beneath the ferment and the cracking, God is at work transforming that which is into that which shall be. Though we walk on the edge of emptiness, we know it is cradled in the fullness of

God. Though we see the froth of life, we know we stand on the Rock of Ages. Though we share the alienation of those who feel lost, we know that even in our despair we are held by a Lover who will never let us go. Though our lives seem fragmented and ineffective, we know that He can gather up the pieces and re-create us according to His purpose. We who live in the time of the end are called to live by "the ethics of the end." The ethics of the end is a threefold imperative which can guide us to reshape our living. "The end of all things is upon us, so you must lead an ordered and sober life, given to prayer."

The ordered life. The ordered life is under the rule of one Lord, who unites our energies, focuses our being, and controls our doing. He organizes and simplifies our life, so that it is like an arrow and not the sprayed bullets of a shotgun. This is a life which is collected, clarified, and reordered. The ordered life is the life of quiet confidence and sustaining inner power. We may ask how the ordering takes place, how we can be effectively receptive to the Lord of order. If freedom is the gift of grace, what are the structures of grace through which the gift is given and received?

Let us consider two structures of grace which are of major importance for the reordering of our lives. The first may be called *the gospel truth,* by which I mean the Bible, holding, as it does, the truth that sets men free. It is just this matter of the truth of the Bible about which many today are uncertain. Christian people are confused about the validity of the biblical witness. Teilhard de Chardin voices a fear of all the faithful when he asks,

Is the Christ of the Gospels, imagined and loved within the dimensions of a Mediterranean world, capable of still embracing and still forming the center of our prodigiously expanding universe? Is the world not in the process of becoming more vast, more close, more dazzling than Jehovah? Will it not burst our religion asunder? Eclipse our God?[9]

Either we hold stubbornly and fiercely to our traditional faith, though unable to articulate it meaningfully to ourselves or outsiders, or we yield to the dilution and relativity of "modern" statements of faith, which usually take the form of either a transcendent or an immanent deism. We are discovering that neither the old fundamentalism, so enamored of gospel truth that it was blind to scientific fact, nor the old liberalism, so enamored of scientific fact that it became uncertain of gospel truth, is adequate for the modern world. A new shape of the gospel must be forged and thought through and lived out—one which will be both true to Christ and relevant to the world.[10]

This means that today's intelligent Christian must undertake the serious and continuing study of the biblical message. Personal confidence can be based only on an intellectually satisfying faith. There are few people who can successfully compartmentalize their faith and derive power from that which they are afraid to test. Large numbers of church members do not know the basic doctrines of faith. The atonement is a stumbling block to many. I am frequently asked in a *koinonia* group, "How could Christ have died for my sins?" The resurrection is quite commonly considered a myth. Those who do not believe in Christ as risen Lord and Savior do not derive the power and freedom brought only by such faith. There must come a theological reformation in the local congregation in which our people are guided to grapple with their own questions and the world's questions. A clear, systematic, authentic Christian theology must be shaped which can enable the concerned Christian to understand himself and the world in biblical perspective.

It takes time to hear the gospel. We have much to unlearn, much misconception to clear away, before we can even begin to hear. A deeply concerned layman who has been a leading member of a leading church for years wrote,

I became aware that I lacked the grounding in Christian beliefs without which no one can be an intelligent, thinking Christian. Such a grounding called for study, not spasmodic attendance at occasional lectures, but regular, disciplined study beginning with the Bible. I began to see that a Christian has a definite responsibility to strive to understand Christ's message, as embodied in His ministry, if he is to enter upon significant discipleship. How easy it is (and how insidious!) to mix together one small portion of Christ's teaching and a large measure of one's own selfish philosophy and thus become a disciple of the status quo, or of rationalized self-interest, or of a special class or race or nationality, all in the guise of "following Christ."

This man recognized the danger of a "little knowledge" of the Bible. The fact that we seldom change our partisan perspectives on politics and economics even after much biblical study indicates how impervious we are to the gospel. This is simply to say that we do not let the gospel easily or quickly penetrate into the basic stance of our life. Pride, prejudice, or privilege yields stubbornly to the gospel truth. Thus, only serious and sustained study holds out hope for the theological undergirding we need. The layman just quoted continues,

It seems to me that to avoid the shoals of shallow thinking, it becomes necessary to refer continually to Chirst's message and ministry as recorded in the New Testament, much as a navigator keeps consulting his compass and charts to make certain that he is on course, and not being deflected by the winds and cross-currents of every passing ideology or movement. This calls for *regular* reading of the Bible and books inspired by it, as well as *regular* prayer, in which God's leading can be sought; in other words, adherence to a discipline.[11]

This leads me to a second structure of grace, which we may call *the life together*. Many readers will recognize in these words the title of Dietrich Bonhoeffer's book, *Life Together*,[12] which is the classic description of all that I wish to say concerning this structure of grace. Life together in Christ is essentially and necessarily corporate. Thus when we talk about "adherence to a discipline" we are speaking of a corporate discipline.

We are all weak, and by ourselves we soon lose our zeal. We need to be bound together in a mutual covenant embodied in concrete disciplines. A group may undertake a fourfold discipline of study, prayer, attendance at regular group meetings, and a specific focus of mission. Corporate study provides enrichment and correction impossible in individual study. The commitment of mutual intercessory prayer means that one belongs to a community of praying friends, giving and receiving spiritual strength far beyond individual capacity alone. Attendance at the group meetings provides face-to-face restoration and renewal of fellowship by means of shared discussion and prayer. The specific focus of mission in the world gives the group its *raison d'être*, turning commitment into concrete service.

Each such group needs to have a system of dealing with failure in the discipline. The great danger is that one may stop making adequate preparation of the study material, or cease praying for group members, or miss a meeting or two without a saving question or challenge from other group members. Such failure in the discipline, unchecked, is like a cancer eating away the integrity of the individual and infecting the entire group. There must be an acceptable and accepted means of acknowledging one's failure and being restored in the fellowship. A group, for example, may study a particular book and then have a special stated meeting before the study of another book begins. At this meeting personal and group appraisal may be offered by group members, personal failings and victories shared, and the mutual covenant reaffirmed in the celebration of Communion. The form of restoration of group fellowship will vary but the need for it is universal.

The greatest weakness of the modern church is its inability to bind and hold people together in concrete covenant. Such a mutual covenant is supposed to be embodied in church-membership vows. But these vows though appropriately worded are usually unrelated to the empty discipleship which prevails. Thus, concerned churchmen find it necessary to seek sustaining power in disciplines of Christian living like those formed at the Kirkridge and Yokefellow Retreat centers. One of the tasks for

theologians in our day is to re-form the norms of church membership which in fact are no longer normative.

It is where two or three are gathered together in Christ's name
that we may best meet the Lord who reconciles us to God and
to one another. For the Word becomes flesh in the love of our
Christian brother, and the message of reconciliation comes alive
in the minister of reconciliation. I have personally experienced
this truth in recent months. I had a matter on my conscience
about which I prayed, asking forgiveness. But I was suspicious
of my prayers and my motivation, and the assurance of forgiveness did not come. It happened that a close friend came for a
day's visit. We spent several hours sailing that day. During the
course of conversation I told him about my lack of assurance
and asked if he would serve as my confessor. He agreed to do
so. I told him in detail the matter of concern. He listened,
questioned me, and then prayed for me. It was a prayer of
absolution, a declaration of forgiveness, the visible and audible
assurance, in a brother who forgives, of the Lord who forgives.
This was a liberating experience for me and in the days that
followed, the assurance of forgiveness *did* come.

The life together is intended to be a life of mutual priesthood,
in which we bear one another's burdens, including the heaviest
burdens of lonely guilt. A man weighed down by guilt is not
free and thus cannot have his life reordered. We need one another in this Christian life in order to forgive and be forgiven,
and so to be set free. We are called together to hear the gospel
and have our lives reshaped by the Lord of order.

The sober life. By "sober" we do not mean puritan or pietistic.
The Christian life is one of joy and freedom, not to be con-
stricted by legalistic rules or expressed in sad countenances. The
sober life is the life responsibly oriented to the world. Its basic
thrust is not frivolous but purposeful. It is no longer aimless but
directed and effective. When we are reordered and regain the
perspective of quiet confidence, we look with new eyes upon our
personal involvements in the world.

The sober life is a *competent* life. In order to make a significant contribution to the world we must be competent in what we seek to do. We need to make a realistic appraisal of our abilities in our particular work and community life. We discover that we cannot be competent in all fields of endeavor, and so we begin to select those that intensify the fruitfulness of our self-investment in church and world.

The sober life is a *focused* life. The necessity for competence means that one must divest himself of peripheral commitments in order to bring energy and attention to bear on the matters of vital concern. One may find himself withdrawing from some of the activities of his church in order that he may concentrate on Bible study and a single mission of the church or on a crucial ministry in some structure of the world. A congregation may determine to re-examine its entire corporate life in the interest of focusing on the two concerns integral to its being—deepening growth in life together, and mission in the immediate community and world. The Christian may find himself withdrawing from a variety of pleasant community associations in order to make an effective, prepared contribution to *one* community need, whether it be public education, or politics, or something else. We need to lay hands of gentle ruthlessness on ourselves, eliminating some things in order to intensify others. It is necessary to prune our lives if they are to bear more fruit.

The sober life is an *urgent* life. This is not the urgency of chronic emergency. It is the quiet, sustained concern to work while it is still day. One who lives the urgent life knows that today is always the day of salvation, decision, significant action, that the time is always short and never certain. His life is charged wth the vigor and purpose of the Spirit. It is the committed life of one who is an army on its mission. This is an urgency which is quietly alert to the opportunities for mission and willing to undergo the disciplines of time, energy, and money required for the accomplishment of the mission. It is an urgency cradled in the abiding confidence that in the Lord our "labour cannot be lost" (I Cor. 15:58, NEB).

A young woman who teaches at a university wrote me about her life and work and unwittingly gave a portrait of the sober life:

Perhaps the most immediate expression of my new concern is my willingness to set aside special periods of time for Bible reading and prayer, regardless of how busy the day may be with academic and social commitments. I find that I also am more willing to interrupt my work to devote time to another person, whether a close friend or a stranger, knowing that God very often has committed someone to my care, and is working through me in that person's life. When confronted with a personal choice among several activities, I usually attempt to consider seriously to which it would be most worthwhile and constructive for me to devote my time. Although I feel that God has chosen particular areas in which I may serve Him, I would not hesitate to change my life work if I believed it were His will. I know that God's ultimate purpose will remain hidden from me, but I trust in His daily guidance, and pray that I may be sensitive and obedient to His direction and that I may find courage to be a true witness of the reality of His presence in my life.

The ordered, sober life, if it is to be sustained, must be a life *given to prayer.* Here is the discipline in which most of us are only beginners, doubtless the one most applauded and least practiced in Christian life. Everybody agrees that he should pray, but few are those who make a serious effort to grow in the knowledge and practice of prayer. We are inclined to think of prayer as one of those things that we just naturally know how to do, and of course in part that is true. But the practice of Christian prayer is not a matter of accident or just "doing what comes naturally."

We need a particular discipline or pattern for effective prayer. I remember being shocked when a respected teacher in a seminary said that he had no set time or period of daily prayer. Surely it is true that a person such as Brother Lawrence, after more than ten years of earnest concentration on the life of prayer, reserved no particular time for prayer; his whole life became suffused with the continual practice of prayer in work and every endeavor. He learned how to worship through his work. Nonetheless I believe that most of us need a pattern of discipline, which will change as we change.

I have found a growing need for waiting quietly on the Lord in my own morning prayer. Perhaps I will read some Scripture or devotional book, and then sit back or kneel and quietly wait. It is like getting the filings of my life reoriented by the magnet of God's love. First He quiets me and clarifies me. Then gradually my priorities are sorted out, and there begin to emerge the things I should do that day, the persons I must see. The assurance comes that this is what He wills, and so I am given the freedom to say "no" to other things without guilt. In waiting prayer I can become independent of, though more sympathetic to, the demands and invitations of others. Often I will write down the names of persons about whom I am concerned, or the appointments and events of the day. This helps to objectify my life so that I can see it in true perspective. I become content to do what *must* be done, and to leave undone that which only *should* be done. Freedom is born in me when I am enabled to accept without guilt the limitations of my energy, time, and competence.

No set pattern or practice of prayer is normative or equally useful for everyone. Indeed, we need to recognize and rejoice in the diversity of disciplines adopted by ourselves and others. Mildred Binns Young has put it well:

. . . each one's discipline must be tailored to his own need, but not tailored by ourselves; rather, in a shop that knows our measurements better than we know them ourselves. Our part is to stand still and let ourselves be fitted. If we are truly fitted, we shall know it and be comfortable. Then we shall not want to complain of or scorn another who wears a different style from the one that has been fitted to us.[13]

A flexibility of discipline allows us to be molded by the Master's hand as He shapes our growing life. Some time ago it occurred to me that my own prayer was overweighted in terms of intercession. I found that I had been spending almost all of my prayer time in concern for other people. It was a kind of horizontal prayer, if you will, directed outward to the neighbor. I recognized that I had been forgetting vertical prayer, the prayer directed in adoration and praise to God Himself. Also in my worthy concern for others I had been glossing over some obvious weaknesses and deficiencies in my own life which needed correction. I had been too willing to accept myself as I was. So I began consciously to give more time to confession and repentance. I deliberately chose devotional readings which spoke to my condition and turned to *The Imitation of Christ*[14] for a proper perspective on my "worldliness." It seems that I need to work through that book every few years so that I am made aware of my limited comprehension of the adoration of God. The saints tell us that adoration of God is the whole content of prayer. And yet I am but a beginner in it. So I must give time to it, cultivate my own adoration of God, read about it, and ask for grace to grow in it.

One of the most helpful books on prayer I have come across in recent years is *Creative Prayer* by E. Herman. She describes the prayer-filled life of St. Philip Neri:

. . . In fine, he took no thought for his spiritual career, but simply exposed himself to God's action upon him day after day, not in an attitude of sterile quietism, but in the spirit of joyous coöperation. And it is little to be wondered at that this quiet, jocund, free-and-easy man, who was so careless about "giving edification," and so utterly detached from everything that was a means and not an end, exercised an almost irresisitible attraction over his contemporaries, winning them from sin and worldliness, subduing their lusts, calming their fears, moulding them to Christian ways, entering into their lives with the transforming ministries of the Gospel, as noiselessly and naturally as the sunlight enters a window at dawn.

The man who is freed from self and has found his true life in God is free indeed. He is untroubled by anxiety even about the affairs of the Kingdom of God. He is never hurried, does not seek place and power, is patient with himself as with others, and takes his faults and failures quietly. There is nothing showy or theatrical about such a man. His life is hid with Christ in God, and hidden from no one more than from himself. . . . The spirit of hiddenness, which . . . is three-fourths of Christianity, and the grace of doing common things in a supernatural way—these are the marks of the man who has been created anew, and prayer which does not stamp these marks upon the soul is greatly to be suspected.[15]

How we long for that single-minded, carefree obedience! When Jesus spoke of the easy yoke (Matt. 11:30), He must have been talking about the surrendered life. Robert Frost has written:

> Something we were withholding made us weak
> Until we found out that it was ourselves
> We were withholding from our land of living,
> And forthwith found salvation in surrender.
> Such as we were we gave ourselves outright.[16]

Our freedom is the freedom of surrender; our order is the order of obedience; our way is the way of a cross.

Conclusion

The Way of a Cross

Bearing the human likeness, revealed in human shape, he humbled himself, and in obedience accepted even death—death on a cross. Therefore God raised him to the heights . . . that at the name of Jesus every knee should bow . . . and every tongue confess, "Jesus Christ is Lord," to the glory of God the Father.

Philippians 2:8-11, NEB

We have sought to discern the shape of Christ in congregational living—as members of His family, as soldiers being equipped in His army, and as His servants and witnesses sent into the world. We have sought to take on the shape of Christ in our personal living—as those aware of His forgiveness, commissioned as agents of His reconciliation, and set free to walk in the spirit of Him who orders our living. We have found a people with whom to walk and a Lord to walk after. He does not give us a convenient set of rules to obey; He is our ruler and we are called to obey Him. He does not give us a map for our pilgrimage; He is the pioneer of our faith and we are to follow Him. We are pilgrims on His way—the way of a cross.

The cross is the sign of Christ's way. It is the sign of Christian living and loving. It is, as Bonhoeffer writes, "the differential of the Christian religion, the power which enables the Christian to transcend the world and to win the victory."[1] The cross marks the beginning of the Christian way, guides its course, and points to its fulfillment.

The way of incarnation. The way of a cross is the way of incarnation. Christ "did not think to snatch at equality with God, but made himself nothing, assuming the nature of a slave" (Phil. 2:6-7, NEB). He voluntarily relinquished His divine status and security and was "revealed in human shape" (Phil. 2:8, NEB). He risked Himself to become personally identified with humanity, involved in the world. He lived a life of unswerving obedience, from the temptation at the beginning of His ministry, through the agony of decision in the Garden of Gethsemane, to the final surrender on the cross. "Father, into thy hands I commit my spirit!" (Luke 23:46).

Christ calls us to follow Him. But we rebel at such obedience. The story of our rebellion is told in the opening chapters of Genesis. Adam and Eve are spiritual antecedents. Like them we refuse to surrender control of our lives to God. We snatch at equality with God and want to rule our own lives. Our natural drive is self-assertion, not submission. We reach out to grasp and eat the apple of success. Success may take different forms in the varieties of human desire, but we are seeking it, hopefully with God's help, but if necessary on our own, and even in defiance of Him.

Christ calls us to follow Him. When the fishermen on the shores of Galilee heard Christ's command, "Follow me," they "left their nets and followed him" (Mark 1:17, 18). They left the security of their old life, the patterns of routine and custom. They relinquished the comforts and accouterments of settled life for a pilgrimage whose destination none knew. No guarantees were given or asked; no conditions were mentioned or questioned. It made no sense by external valuation. Yet they followed Him.

Christ calls us to let go the nets in which we are comfortably caught—the customs, conventions, and circumstances of our lives. Christ calls us to let go the web of our securities, to disentangle ourselves from the tentacles of secondary involvements to be free to follow wherever He leads us. When Christ calls, we struggle and resist. We are afraid of venturing forth from all that we know, understand, and can control into that which we do not know, do not understand, and cannot control. We know that when we pull up our social, psychological, and religious anchors we will find ourselves at sea, no longer in control, literally at His mercy. So we make excuses. We say, "I'm too old to change . . . I'm too busy to get involved . . . I have to buy a house and raise my family and work at my job . . . Not now, but next month, next year . . ."

How human it is to settle into the warm and comforting womb of our life, which in truth is already becoming the tomb of our death. For life that settles in is life that is on its way out. Teilhard de Chardin speaks to our condition:

An honest workman not only surrenders his tranquillity and peace once and for all, but must learn to abandon over and over again the form which his labour or art or thought first took, and go in search of new forms. To pause, so as to enjoy or possess results, would be a betrayal of action. Over and over again he must transcend himself, tear himself away from himself, leaving behind him his most cherished beginnings. And on that road, which is not so different from the royal road of the Cross as might appear at first sight . . . each reality attained and left behind gives us access to the discovery and pursuit of an ideal of higher spiritual content. Those who spread their sails in the right way to the winds of the earth will always find themselves borne by a current towards the highest seas. . . . So, gradually the worker no longer belongs to himself. Little by little the great breath of the universe has insinuated itself into him through the fissure of his humble but faithful action, has broadened him, raised him up, borne him on.[2]

Here is the promise that those who take "the royal road of the Cross" will find a sustaining Power and Presence for their pilgrimage. It is the same promise first given to Abraham, who obeyed the call of God, and "went out, not knowing where he was to go" (Heb. 11:8). It is the call to discipleship in every age. And "if we answer the call to discipleship, where will it lead us?

What decisions and partings will it demand? To answer this question, we shall have to go to Him, for only He knows the answer. Only Jesus Christ, who bids us follow Him, knows the journey's end. But we do know that it will be a road of boundless mercy. Discipleship means joy."[3]

The way of incarnation is God's way toward fulfillment. Only as we risk ourselves can we find ourselves. Only as we lose our lives can our lives be saved. We are sent into the world, the world which God loves, the world for which Christ died and was raised. Salvation is not to be found out of this world, but precisely in its grandeur and misery, for it is God's purpose to save the world (John 3:17).

The way of atonement. The way of a cross is the way of atonement. It is God's personal way of suffering with and for humanity in order that we might be reconciled to Him and to one another. The scope and dimension of Christ's sacrificial love appear in the words "he humbled himself, and in obedience accepted even death—death on a cross." In Hebrews we read that "although he was a Son, he learned obedience through what he suffered...," and that it was the purpose of God to "make the pioneer of ... salvation perfect through suffering" (Heb. 5:8, 2:10). It is significant that the one word in the Apostles' Creed which defines the substance of Christ's living is the word "suffered."

Christ endured personal suffering. He suffered the misunderstanding of family and friends and the betrayal of his followers. His physical and spiritual suffering in the course of His ministry find ultimate expression on the cross. "I thirst" (John 19:28) is the word of man's physical need. "My God, my God, why hast thou forsaken me?" (Mark 15:34) is the word of man's spiritual despair.

Christ suffered with and for humanity. He had "compassion" on crowds (Matt. 9:36, Mark 6:34) and on individuals (Luke 7:13). Compassion means literally "to suffer with." One can have pity on another at a distance, but one can have compassion on another only by deliberately becoming involved in the suffering of the other. It is no coincidence that in the two greatest of Christ's parables the key word is "compassion." The father of the Prodigal Son "had compassion" on him and ran to forgive him (Luke 15:20). The Good Samaritan "had compassion" on the beaten man lying on the road and stopped to help him (Luke 10:33). Compassion is to suffer on behalf of the neighbor and even the enemy. Christ's compassion finds its ultimate expression on the cross in the words "Father, forgive them; for they know not what they do" (Luke 23:34).

Christ calls us to suffer. He calls us to endure our personal suffering in the knowledge that God is in it with us. Forbes Robinson sent a letter to a friend whose brother had been killed by lightning. He wrote,

I can only tell you what I have felt to be the only thing which makes life endurable at a time of real sorrow—God himself. He comes unutterably near in trouble. In fact, one hardly knows He exists until one loves or sorrows. There is no "getting over " sorrow. . . . But there is a "getting into" sorrow and finding right in the heart of it—the Man of Sorrows, a God. . . . I pray that you may never "get over" the sorrow but get through it, into it, into the very heart of God.[4]

All human suffering, nobly borne, has redemptive significance. Harper Lee, in her novel *To Kill a Mockingbird*, describes a sick woman, Mrs. Dubose, who took morphine as a pain-killer. As the last months of her life drew nigh, she had become a morphine addict. She could have taken the drug to the very end, being as free of pain as possible under the circumstances. But she was determined to break the addiction and not be beholden to anything and anybody when she died. So she endured the agony of not having the drug, but by the time of her death, she had freed herself of the addiction. During the final months of Mrs. Dubose's illness a man sent his son to read to her to help her pass the hours away. It was a disagreeable task because she was cantankerous, rude, and ungrateful. When she died, the father explained to his son why he had sent him to read to Mrs. Dubose:

I wanted you to see something about her—I wanted you to see what real courage is, instead of getting the idea that courage is a man with a gun in his hand. It's when you know you're licked before you begin but you begin anyway and you see it through no matter what. You rarely win, but sometimes you do. Mrs. Dubose won, all ninety-eight pounds of her. According to her views, she died beholden to nothing and nobody. She was the bravest person I ever knew.[5]

The witness of such suffering rebukes and encourages us in the bearing of our own burdens. Such suffering is not for naught but speaks to us of the suffering love of God. Although Christ calls us to suffer with and for humanity, to have compassion, we recoil from this personal involvement. We would rather withdraw from the dirt and sorrow of human misery. Some time ago I was driving out of the slum section of a city to the suburbs and stopped at a red light. As I waited for the light to turn green, my eye happened to fall upon a man standing on the corner. There was something the matter with him. He was ragged and unkempt, his eyes were rolling, his mouth was hanging open with saliva drooling from it. He was a human wreck. I saw him, and the moment the light turned green pressed compulsively on the accelerator to get away as fast as I could from this man by the side of the road. I was unwilling to have compassion on him.

In innumerable ways we excuse and forgive ourselves for our unwillingness to become involved in the sufferings of others. Some of us have compassion on individuals but not on crowds; we may take great pains to help a single unfortunate case but never see individual faces of need in a crowd.

It is often the political conservative who has compassion on the individual but not on crowds, just as it is often the political liberal who is so caught up in his vision for the welfare of all mankind that he has little time to consider individual needs along the way. Christ calls us to have compassion on crowds and individuals.

We indulge in vicarious compassion. Some time ago *Life* magazine[6] portrayed a heart-rending picture story of the poverty and sickness of a South American child. The response of the reader-

ship to this picture of human need was amazing. Letters and
checks poured in for the child, and there was widespread re-
joicing when the youngster was brought to this country for
medical help and rehabilitation. I wondered at the time how many
of those who felt so moved by this human suffering far away in
another country realized that only a few miles from their own
homes in the slums of every major American metropolitan area
this story of human misery could be written a thousand times
over. Such compassion-at-a-distance can be a cover for our unwillingness to have compassion on those near at hand. Near-at-
hand compassion requires the risk and cost of personal involvement. But it is precisely to such involvement in the sufferings of
the weak and disadvantaged people within our own sphere of influence that we are called. Suburban and urban Christians are
responsible for the healing and renewal of their own metropolitan
area.

The way of resurrection. The way of a cross is the way of
resurrection—"Therefore God raised him to the heights . . ."
(Phil. 2:9, NEB). Death means deliverance; the old creation is
covered by a new creation. The final word on the cross, "It is
finished" (John 19:30), sounds the knell of the old order and
opens a new and living way for all men. It is the Easter way of
joy and victory.

Christ calls us to rejoice: "These things I have spoken to you,
that my joy may be in you, and that your joy may be full"
(John 15:11). Christ calls us to rejoice in His living presence.
Even now we know the power of His resurrection through the
church which is His body. He lives as our Lord and Savior where
two or three are gathered together in His name. We know Him
in the joy of a new companionship, the vigor and vitality of a
new and holy Spirit. Like the first disciples, we are witnesses to
His resurrection (Acts 2:32) in our own lives.

But what do we mean by the presence of the risen Christ in us?
Ours is a generation which finds it difficult to be sure of His
presence. We hear a verse of that favorite gospel song of our

parents or grandparents, "In the Garden": "He walks with me
and he talks with me and he tells me I am his own. . . ." But it
doesn't describe our experience. Few of us have such individual
awareness of His presence. The song leaves us shaking our heads
and wondering if Christ really is present in our lives. We want
Him to be present, but we don't feel anything special which
would denote His presence. Indeed, we distrust our emotions
anyway and wonder whether we *should* feel anything special to
signify His presence. What we may genuinely be aware of is a
sense of the remoteness of Christ, the blurred memory of a man
we never knew, colored by the fantasies of childhood, shrouded
in the darkness of our own uncertainty.

A friend of mine became mentally ill and spent several periods
of time in a mental hospital. He wrote me about his experience:

When I was put in "solitary"—a room about ten feet by ten feet,
with only an eight-inch-square window in the door, with a pattern
of wire in the glass so that you couldn't break it—I felt the absence
of Christ—the most lost feeling humanly possible, completely alone.
I tried praying, but felt even He wasn't listening. I lived with just
myself for days. The only time I saw anybody was at mealtime, and
then only for a split second. After some time, I started to feel like
a pitcher being filled with forgiveness for my past sins, and a surging
power came. I stayed in the cell, but it was as though the door were
unlocked and opened.

Christ is with us in the darkness, and especially there. He is no
stranger to the valley of shadows. He has walked there himself.
He too has cried out, "Why hast thou forsaken me?" He knows;
He understands; He cares. Though we cannot see Him through
the clouds of doubt and despair, His light shines—light which no
darkness can extinguish.

When we are personally beaten or broken, and Christ seems
far away from us, we are given to know His love in the presence
of our brothers and sisters in Christ. Years ago a friend of mine
lost his wife by drowning. It was sheer tragedy. I wrote him a
letter, saying the things one says in such a letter. In time it was

answered by a poignant expression of Christian faith, an Easter cry on the day after Good Friday.

The absurd worst has happened. She who stood at the center of my life walks with me no more. Without any warning the news came. She is gone! She died saving the life of our youngest. Like a vine fallen to the ground when the tree around which it is entwined is uprooted—so I fell.

Now I know the meaning of that Good Friday cry as it wells up from the center of my own being. My soul is like a storm-swept, barren desert where violent winds blow—questionings, despair, loneliness, anger, emptiness, and fierce longing. And it is dark. But as these winds blow and I experience the dark night of the soul, I know that there is oil in my lamp. Esther and I are not in any way separated from the love of God. We are together in His care, and His grace is sufficient. In these days I have found great comfort in the fellowship of the Beloved Community in Christ. It is a bright reality to me. I thank you for your loving concern which has strengthened and helped to uphold me. Please continue to pray for me, for I am in great need . . . "left wounded and half-dead by the road." Pray that God will raise me up and give me courage to do what I ought.

As he groped and stumbled through the following weeks and months, he sensed that he was being upheld by his Christian friends, and through them by the everlasting arms of God Himself. And there came a looking back in memory and a looking forward in hope which gave impetus to his lonely journey and filled with new and eternal significance the life they shared and the reunion toward which they move. He wrote,

Esther and I were very close. She was my wife, the mother of my children, my dearest friend, my fellow pilgrim in the Christian way. She it was in whom I delighted most and in whose presence I would rather be than any other. Together we searched out life's meanings and celebrated them over and over again. . . . In our love we discerned the love of God. She was a pilgrim and as a pilgrim she went through the gates. And so I believe she continues with glad, thankful surprise at the wonders of heaven.

But we do not yet know the grave or the skies. Our way is still the way of the cross, the way of living by faith through love, in hope.

The way of consummation. The way of a cross is the way of consummation. It is the way to ultimate completion of God's work in the world, and the total fulfillment of God's purpose in Christ. The consummation is that time when "at the name of Jesus every knee should bow—in heaven, on earth, and in the depths— and every tongue confess, 'Jesus Christ is Lord,' to the glory of God the Father" (Phil. 2:11, NEB). It is the time when the lion shall lie down with the lamb, the time of the new heaven and the new earth. It is the time when time itself shall be transfigured into eternity, and all things be brought into a unity in Christ. It is what we refer to as the "Second Coming" of Christ, the Christ who says, "I am coming soon." We do not know what is coming, but we do know Who is coming. We live now in between the time of the great Easter deliverance and the time of ultimate freedom (I Pet. 1:3, 13). We live in the certainty of hope expressed in one of Dietrich Bonhoeffer's last letters, written from his prison cell just before his execution. He wrote,

> Please don't ever get anxious or worried about me, but don't forget to pray for me—I'm sure you don't! I am so sure of God's guiding hand, and I hope I shall never lose that certainty. You must never doubt that I am traveling my appointed road with gratitude and cheerfulness. My past life is replete with God's goodness, and my sins are covered by the forgiving love of Christ crucified. I am thankful for all those who have crossed my path, and all I wish is never to cause them sorrow, and that they, like me, will always be thankful for the forgiveness and mercy of God and sure of it. Please don't for a moment get upset by all this, but let it rejoice in your heart.[8]

The way of Christ is the way of a cross, that cross beneath which "two wonders I confess, the wonders of redeeming love and my unworthiness."[9]

There it is—God's redeeming love and our unworthiness. Our way is the way of penitence to the very end. It is the way of taking up our cross daily, praying to the Lord to give us this day our daily bread and forgive us this day our daily trespasses. Martin Luther wrote toward the end of his life,

Our good is hidden and that so deep that it is hidden under its very contrary. Thus our life is hidden under death, our joy under hatred, glory under shame, salvation under perdition, the Kingdom under exile, heaven under hell, wisdom under foolishness, righteousness under sin, strength under infirmity.[10]

Yet our way is the way of exaltation from the beginning. For we live in the grace of a redeeming love which lifts us up beyond ourselves. We look up to Him who said, "and I, when I am lifted up from the earth, will draw all men to myself" (John 12:32). We are drawn, yea borne up, by Him, raised with Him to reign with Him. For He is crowned King of kings, there, on the cross. The angel voices sing and sing, "Crown Him with many crowns, the Lamb upon His throne."[11] All the company of heaven and earth sing,

> Alleluia:
> For the Lord God omnipotent reigneth.
> Alleulia!
> The kingdoms of this world are become the
>   kingdoms of our Lord, and of his Christ;
>   and he shall reign for ever and ever.
> King of kings, and Lord of lords.
> Alleluia![12]

Appendix 1.   Bible Study Outlines

The purpose of the study outlines offered here is to provide concrete guides for the use of study groups, in or outside the church, with or without clergy leadership. The number of sessions for each book of the Bible can be decreased or increased depending on the time and specific purpose of the study. The procedure with regard to the questions raised is to determine the meaning of the biblical passage first, then its implications for personal and congregational life and work. This is what may be called a "Word and Word-become-flesh" approach. It is suggested that some commentary be used to aid private study in preparation for the group meetings.

The Gospel of Mark

Session I.
    Read Mark 1.
    Questions: How does Jesus' unique personal authority manifest itself in His impact on the fishermen and on the people in the synagogue? What is His impact on you?

Session II.
    Read Mark 2:1-3:6:
    Questions: In five episodes here Jesus antagonizes the religious leaders. Why is He a threat to them? Is He a threat to you? Why? Why not?

Session III.
    Read Mark 3:7-4:34
    Questions: What is Jesus' concept of the Kingdom of God?

Are you aware of the reign of God in your life, and in the lives of others known to you?

Session IV.

Read Mark 4:35-6:32

Questions: How does the power of Christ work in relation to the disciples in the boat, the Gerasene demoniac, the woman with the chronic illness, the daughter of Jairus, and the people of His home town? What is your personal knowledge of the power of Christ, or lack of it, in your own life?

Session V.

Read Mark 6:33-8:30

Questions: What is Mark affirming about the sufficiency of Christ to meet man's needs in the feeding stories, and later in the event of the Lord's Supper? (Mark 14:17 ff.) What do you believe about Christ's sufficiency to meet your daily needs? What is the meaning of the Lord's Supper to you?

Session VI.

Read Mark 8:31-10:52

Questions: What is Jesus' concept of discipleship? Is this what your church says about discipleship to its present members? In its new-member training? How does your own concrete discipleship measure up?

Session VII.

Read Mark 11-13

Questions: What is the significance of the cleansing of the temple for the religion of Jesus' day? For our own religion? What is the meaning of the Second Coming of Christ?

Session VIII.

Read Mark 14-16

Questions: Why did Jesus have to die? Do you believe He died for you? What happened in the resurrection? Do you believe Christ is risen in your life?

The Acts of the Apostles*

Session I.

Read Acts 1-2

* Many of the ideas for this outline given by John Lynn Carr, pastor of the Church of the Savior, Indianapolis, Indiana.

Theme: The Holy Spirit creates a new community (the church).

Questions: What are the signs of the Spirit's presence in this new community? (See 2:41-47.) Are there similar signs of the Spirit's presence in your congregation?

Session II.

Read Acts 3-5

Theme: The Spirit-filled community is a witnessing community.

Questions: To what and to whom did the early Christians regard themselves as witnesses? (Check the burden of Peter's sermons: 2:14-36; 3:12-26; 5:30-32.) Are you and the people of your church a witnessing community? How can a modern congregation make effective witness?

Session III.

Read Acts 6-9

Theme: The Spirit changes your life.

Questions: How did the Spirit change Paul? (Note the accounts of Paul's conversion in Acts 9:1-9; 22:4-16; 26:9-18, and Galatians 1:11-17.) Have you been or are you being changed by the Spirit? In work context, in regard to movements for social justice and peace, in political involvement?

Session IV.

Read Acts 10-20

Theme: On receiving and rejecting the Spirit.

Questions: If a neighbor or associate at work asked you the question of the Philippian jailer (16:30)—that is, how to receive the Spirit—what would you say to him? What causes people to ask or not to ask such questions of us? What are some of the reasons why Paul's message is rejected? (16:16-24; 17:1-9; 19:23-41.) Can you think of circumstances today where we reject the Spirit for reasons of national, political, economic, or personal vested interests?

Session V.

Read Acts 21-28.

Theme: The Spirit guides your living.

Questions: We marvel at the joy and assurance of the Spirit's leading characteristic of the early church. Can we know such firsthand leading in our own living? How

can we become more sensitive to the Spirit? Are
there any tests to distinguish between the Spirit and
our own thoughts?

Session VI.

Reread Acts in its entirety.

Theme: The Spirit at work in your congregation.

Questions: What are the barriers to the Spirit's effective work
in your congregation? What can you do to prepare
the way for the Spirit's presence and power in your
congregation?

First Corinthians

Read Acts 18:1-18, a narrative of the founding of the Corinthian
Church.

Session I.

Read I Cor. 1

Questions: What is Paul's concept of the cross? What is yours?
Is it primarily a stumbling block or sheer nonsense to
you? Do you think that God more or less con-
sistently chooses people who are not "wise" or
"powerful" according to worldly standards through
whom to do His work in the world? (1:26 ff.)

Session II.

Read I Cor. 2-4

Questions: What is this "secret and hidden wisdom of God"?
(2:7.) Who are "unspiritual" and "spiritual" men,
and how are they to be discerned? (2:14-16.) Where
are you at present in terms of Paul's discussion of
Christians as "men of the flesh," "babes in Christ,"
"spiritual men"? Have you any personal experience
of being regarded as a fool "for Christ's sake"?
(4:10.)

Session III.

Read I Cor. 5-7

Questions: What does it mean to "glorify God in your body"?
(6:20.) What does it mean to give "your undivided
devotion to the Lord"? (7:35.) Does Paul advise the
Corinthian Christians to shun the company of obvious sinners who are inside the church or outside
the church? Why? What does it mean to live an "as
though . . . not" (7:29-31) kind of life?

Session IV.
 Read I Cor. 8-11:1
 Questions: What does it mean to be your brother's keeper?
 (8:13, 10:23-11:1.) What does Paul mean when he
 speaks of being "all things to all men"? (9:22.) What
 is Paul's concept of Christian freedom in these
 chapters? (10:23-26.)

Session V.
 Read I Cor. 11
 Questions: What does Paul mean by saying that by eating the
 bread and drinking the cup we proclaim the Lord's
 death till He comes? (11:26) What does it mean to
 partake of the Lord's Supper "in an unworthy manner," or "without discerning the body"? (11:27-32)

Session VI.
 Read I Cor. 12
 Questions: What is Paul's concept of the nature of our belonging
 to Christ and to one another? How is the variety of
 gifts constituted and expressed in the body of Christ?
 How in your congregation can people be grafted into
 the body and enabled to give their gifts?

Session VII.
 Read I Cor. 13
 Questions: What is the most striking aspect of Paul's picture of
 Christian love? What are the implications of this kind
 of love for marriage, parent-child relationships, re-
 lationships at work, and in the wider community?

Session VIII.
 Read I Cor. 14
 Questions: What is speaking in tongues, as Paul describes it?
 Do you have any personal knowledge of it in our
 time? What things are essential in worship according
 to Paul? (14:26 ff.) What are the implications in the
 order of worship in your church?

Session IX.
 Read I Cor. 15
 Questions: What does Paul mean by a "spiritual body"? (15:44)
 Does Paul affirm the resurrection of the dead or the
 resurrection of the body? (15:42) What do you
 make of the fact that Paul puts his own confrontation
 by the risen Christ on a par with that of the disciples

(using the same verb "appeared" to describe it)?
(15:3-8) What is the "mystery" (15:51) of which
Paul speaks? What are the dimensions of the "victory" (15:57) God has won by the resurrection?

Session X.
Read I Cor. 16
Questions: What is Paul's interpretation of Christian giving in
this chapter? What are the implications for the giving program in your church? What are the implications of the house-churches Paul refers to, for your
congregational life together?

Second Corinthians

Session I.
Read II Cor. 1
Questions: What does it mean to "share . . . Christ's sufferings"?
(1:5 ff.) Have you known God's comfort most
strongly in times of suffering, or not? What does
Paul mean by saying that the "promises of God" find
their "yes" in Christ?

Session II.
Read II Cor. 2
Questions: How do you deal with one who is failing in his Christian life in your congregation? What are the procedures for the priesthood of all believers in your
church?

Session III.
Read II Cor. 3
Questions: In Paul's thought what is the difference between
self-confidence and confidence in God through
Christ? Is it wrong to have self-confidence? What
does it mean for your church that "you are a letter
from Christ" (3:3) addressed to your community?
What would it mean for you and for your church
to be "changed into his likeness"? (3:18)

Session IV.
Read II Cor. 4
Questions: In what way is the gospel "veiled"? (4:3) Who or
what blinds the minds of unbelievers, and even believers? According to Paul, why is it that "we do
not lose heart"? (4:1, 16)

Session V.

  Read II Cor. 5

  Questions: What does it mean to be controlled by the love of
               Christ? (5:14) What does it mean that one has "died
               for all"? (5:14) How does the "human point of
               view" differ from the Christian point of view? (5:16)
               In our time where do you see God reconciling peo-
               ple—in family life, where you work, in racial con-
               flict, in international relations? Are you and your
               church involved in God's reconciling ministry?

Session VI.

  Read II Cor. 6

  Questions: Is Paul's experience (6:3-10) characteristic of Chris-
               tian experience in our time? What does it mean to
               "accept the grace of God in vain"? (6:1) What are
               the implications for you and your church of Jesus'
               words: "Blessed are those who are persecuted. . . .
               Woe to you, when all men speak well of you"?
               (Matt. 5:10, Luke 6:26)

Session VII.

  Read II Cor. 7

  Questions: Are we to expect trials and suffering as Christians?
               Does some suffering come to us because we are
               Christians? What is the difference between "worldly"
               and "godly" grief? (7:10)

Session VIII.

  Read II Cor. 8-9

  Questions: What does Paul mean by associating the giving of
               money and the giving of self to the Lord? (8:3-5)
               What does it mean to give "according to their means"
               and "beyond their means"? (8:3) What are the im-
               plications for the giving appeal and program in your
               church? Does 8:8-15 have any implications for the
               welfare state?

Session IX.

  Read II Cor. 10-12

  Questions: What do you make of Paul's "boasting"? How do
               you understand Paul's revelation experience? (12:1
               ff.) What does it mean that God's power is made
               perfect in weakness, and that when I am weak, then
               I am strong? (12:9, 10) What are the "signs of a true
               apostle"? (12:12)

Session X.

Read II Cor. 13

Questions: How do you and the people of your church "Examine yourselves, to see whether you are holding to your faith"? (13:5) What would such a self-inventory include? Where in your Christian faith and life do you especially need help, correction, encouragement, strength?

Galatians

Session I. (grace)

Read Gal. 1-2

Questions: What is Paul's concept of grace? How does such grace affect your work structures and relationships, your family relationships, your participation in the wider community? Thus, what does it mean to be a gracious wife, sister, husband, parent, employer, citizen? How can one work for a "gracious" world community? What is the cost of such "gracious living"?

Session II. (faith)

Read Gal. 3

Questions: What is Paul's concept of faith? (3:23-29) Why can't we be justified by works, or by obedience to law? What is the valid function of law (Ten Commandments, etc.) in our relationship with God? What does it mean to live by faith in your daily work, in your participation in the wider community? What does "hearing with faith" mean? (3:5)

Session III. (freedom)

Read Gal. 4-5:15

Questions: What is the Christian free from (independence), free to (dependence), free for (interdependence)? (5:13-14) What does it mean thus to be a free man in daily work, in family life, in working for a "gracious" world community? What structure of discipline (not arbitrary rules) can support and sustain this freedom?

Session IV. (life in the Spirit)

Read Gal. 5:16-6

Questions: What is your experience of the conflict between flesh

and Spirit? (5:16 ff.) Are the fruits of the Spirit
evident in any respect where you work, in those who
are not Christians, in family life? What is your
understanding and experience of Christian burden-
bearing? (6:1-5)

Galatians 2:20 is a key passage in the New Testament. Write a
brief essay giving your interpretation of its meaning for you.

Ephesians

Session I.
  Read Eph. 1
  Questions: What is God's mission or purpose in the world?
             (1:10) Why and how has God made known "the
             mystery of his will" to us (Christians)? (1:9) Why
             have we been chosen and not somebody else? What
             is "the hope to which he has called you . . . his
             glorious inheritance"? (1:18)

Session II.
  Read Eph. 2
  Questions: What is the death and the life of which Paul speaks
             in 2:1-5? What does it mean to be "saved" "by
             grace . . . through faith . . . created in Christ Jesus
             for good works"? (2:8-10) What are the dividing
             walls of hostility which God would break down in
             our time? What does it mean in family, work,
             intergroup, and international relationships for the
             church of Christ to preach and make peace?
             (2:11-22)

Session III.
  Read Eph. 3-4:16
  Questions: What is the purpose of the church? What is the
             "mystery" of Christ? (3:4) What is the distinguish-
             ing character of the life together in Christ? (4:1-16)
             By what standard can we determine what is essential
             and what is peripheral in the ways we spend time
             together as Christians?

Session IV.
  Read Eph. 4:17-6:9
  Questions: What does it mean to put off the old nature and put
             on the new nature? How can we help one another

to do this? (4:22-24) What does it mean to "walk in love," as Paul describes it? (5:1-20) What are the admonitions for marriage, family life, and work given by Paul? (5:21-6:9) Do you agree with his counsel?

Session V.

Read Eph. 6:10 to the end.

Questions: What does it mean for your church to be an out-post of the army of the Lord and you a soldier of Christ on mission in the world? Who is our greatest enemy? What sort of armor as protection does Paul recommend?

Appendix 2. Midweek Luncheon Club*

PURPOSE: To promote mutual understanding and to introduce spiritual motivation in employee relationships.

FORM: Lunch—15 minutes.

Reading—5 minutes.

Silent Meditation, contemplation, prayer—5 minutes (initially 1 or 2 minutes until group is sized up, but provide the time, even though short, so it does not have to be introduced as a new idea later).

Discussion }
Questions } 35 minutes

Session I.

Purpose: To get to know each other.

Reading: Joseph A. Breig, "Three Types of People," *Catholic Digest*, Jan. 1954 (an article describing people as oriented primarily to things, ideas, or people).

Leading questions: What circumstances brought you to work here? Tell us about your family, your hobbies, your organizational interests.

Session II.

Purpose: To reveal religious philosophy of each member of the group.

Reading: Psalm 8; excerpts from "Give Me Liberty or Give Me Death" speech of Patrick Henry; two opening paragraphs of the Declaration of Independence.

Leading questions: What is man? Who are you?

* Outline prepared by Dr. Edwin C. Dreby, Scholler Bros., Inc., Philadelphia, Pa.

Session III.

    Purpose: To explore the concept of "work" in the life of man.

    Reading: Genesis 1, 2; Douglas Steere, *Work and Contemplation* (New York: Harper & Row, 1957), Chapter 1.

    Leading questions: What is work? What is the purpose of work?

Session IV.

    Purpose: To discuss those qualities in relationships between a group that result in the development of a team or bring about teamwork.

    Reading: Romans 12, 13.

    Leading questions: What is a team? What relationships must exist to make an effective team?

Session V.

    Purpose: To explore team organization—coach, captain, member relationships.

    Reading: Brice Durbin, *How to Create Team Spirit* (Montclair, N.J.: Portrait Publications, Economics Press, Inc., 1951).

    Leading questions: What functions do the parts of the organization serve? What moral responsibilities do each have for each other?

Session VI.

    Purpose: To discuss multi-team relationships as in a company.

    Reading: John Luther, *What Difference Does It Make* (Montclair, N.J.: Economics Press, Inc., 1960).

Session VII.

    Purpose: To explore a company's role in society.

    Reading: Selections from Chaps. 1 and 8 in R. L. Howe, *The Creative Years* (Greenwich, Conn.: The Seabury Press, 1959).

Session VIII

    Purpose: To discuss the nature of and fulfillment for man in a work situation.

    Reading: Douglas Steere, *Work and Contemplation* (New York: Harper & Row, 1957), Chap. 8.

    Leading questions: What conditions must exist in a worker's attitude toward his work to bring joy and satisfaction?

    What kind of work situation allows for exercise of creativity at all levels?

Session IX.

    Purpose: To evaluate previous sessions and open floor for discussion of future sessions.

Reading: C. S. Lewis, *Screwtape Letters* (Glasgow: Fontana
Books, William Collins Sons and Company, 1955),
Chap. 3.

Questions: During previous sessions be sensitive to expressions
spritual in nature so that moves can be made in this
direction.

Be alert to phases of previous subjects that are revealed as of particular interest and suitable for further
discussion.

Appendix 3. Outline of Five Premarital Counseling Sessions*

PURPOSES: 1. To establish an open, supportive relationship between pastor and engaged couple which will put wedding ceremony in context of greater understanding, appreciation, and sacredness, and will make postmarital counseling more acceptable if and as needed.
2. To help engaged persons to clarify their understanding of themselves and their needs, and the nature of the marriage relationship itself.
3. To relieve feelings of guilt and anxiety which might be involved in the situation for either person.

PLACE AND TIME: Five hourly sessions, weekly, in the minister's study.

Session I. (introduction)

10 minutes A. Discussion of where and how couple met, how long they've known each other.

30 minutes B. Discussion of general wedding plans, including time and date of wedding, rehearsal, wedding music, pictures, attendants, reception, etc.
1. This gives opportunity to observe attitudes and feeling of couple both about marriage and about each other.
2. Enables minister to clarify meaning of service and answer questions early to avoid future misunderstanding.

---

*Prepared by Theodore W. Loder, co-minister of the First Methodist Church, Germantown, Philadelphia, Pennsylvania.

15 minutes   C. Ask couple to fill out Background Schedule, an information sheet with pertinent facts about self, family, interests, partner. This information provides material for use in future sessions.

5 minutes   D. Outline subjects for future discussion, selected because they are the areas most frequently involved in marital difficulty. Give them one of the books listed below.

      E. Closing prayer and Lord's Prayer.

Session II. (Finances)

10 minutes   A. Review wedding plans and answer questions.

35 minutes   B. Introduce subject with discussion of couple's plans for a place to live, whether furnished, transportation needs, etc.

        1. Ask about backgrounds of families, fathers' vocations, etc., using Background Schedule sheet.

        2. Discuss what the couple consider to be their material needs, and how they propose to provide for them. Discuss budgeting.

        3. Discuss the man's vocation—why chosen, present development, future expectations as related to income. If woman is working, explore what this means psychologically as well as financially.

15 minutes   C. Discuss relationship between financial attitudes and life goals.

        1. Inquire about their basis for deciding between essential and nonessential needs.

        2. Stress importance of mutuality in financial decision making.

      D. Closing prayer and Lord's Prayer.

Session III. (Families and in-laws)

5 minutes   A. Review wedding plans and answer questions.

35 minutes   B. Introduce subject with discussion concerning parents' attitudes about their forthcoming marriage.

        1. Discuss relationships between them and parents prior to this time, using Background Schedule sheet. Also relations with brothers and sisters, or other primary family figures.

2. Discuss geographical proximity of newly-weds' home to that of parents, and why, and anticipated frequency of visits, etc.

3. Explore how long each has known the other's parents, how well they've gotten along, what they consider to be an ideal relationship with in-laws and own parents.

20 minutes   C. Explore their attitudes about the relative importance of their marriage relationship, and their feelings about independence and dependence on families. Discuss their feelings about how their new relationship is affecting and will affect their future relationships with parents and in-laws, and what part these feelings will play in their marriage, and how they might handle them.

D. Closing prayer and Lord's Prayer.

Session IV. (Sexual adjustment)

5 minutes   A. Review wedding plans and answer questions.

30 minutes   B. Introduce subject with discussion about family planning. (Use Family Life Sex Knowledge Inventory if desirable—see below.)

1. Inquire whether couple has had recent physical examinations, and whether they have gotten medical advice regarding contraception.

2. Tell couple that misinformation about sex is not uncommon and causes much heartache that can be avoided.

3. Inquire about their educational background in biology or related field. Discuss biological factors in sexual relations, based on their reading. (See below.)

25 minutes   C. Discuss psychological factors in sexual adjustment.

1. Stress basic importance of sexual fulfillment in strong marriage, and need for patient persistence in working toward it.

2. Help couple clarify common psychological hurdles to be overcome toward such fulfillment.

D. Closing prayer and Lord's Prayer.

Session V. (Christian marriage) (It is desirable that this session be as
close as possible to the rehearsal.)

10 minutes   A. Discuss religious development of each person,
using Background Sheet.

20 minutes   B. Discuss the Service of Matrimony—the word-
ing, the vows and their meaning.

30 minutes   C. Discuss the place of the church in marriage and
the home, and the couple's plans regarding it.

1. Discuss attitudes toward prayer, Bible reading, public worship.

2. Suggest relationship between faith in God
and their understanding of life's purpose.

D. Give them George W. Brown's book *Your First
Week Together,* and perhaps also *Prayer and
Personal Religion* by John Coburn.

E. Closing prayer and Lord's Praper.

Bibliography

I. THE MINISTER'S PREPARATION

Annette Garret. *Interviewing: Its Principles and Methods.* Family
Service Association of America, 192 Lexington Ave., New
York 16, N. Y.

J. K. Morris. *Premarital Counseling—A Manual for Ministers.*
Englewood Cliffs, N.J.: Prentice-Hall, 1960.

James A. Peterson. *Toward a Successful Marriage.* New York:
Charles Scribner's Sons, 1960.

Judge Louis H. Burke. *With This Ring.* New York: McGraw-
Hill Book Company, 1958.

Erich Fromm. *The Art of Loving.* New York: Harper & Row,
1956.

The Encyclopedia of Sexual Behavior, Vols. I and II, selected
articles. (Ellis and Abarbanel, editors.) New York: Hawthorn
Books, Inc., 1961.

Arthur M. Tingue. "The Minister's Role in Marriage Preparation
and Premarital Counseling," *Marriage and Family Living,* February 1958, Vol. XX, No. 1. Reprint from American Foundation of Religion and Psychology.

H. Bowman. *Marriage for Moderns.* New York: McGraw-Hill
Book Company,

Nathan Ackerman. *The Psycho-Dynamics of Family Life.* New
York: Basic Books, Inc.

II. USEFUL MATERIALS FOR FACT FINDING (mentioned above)

Background Schedule Sheet. Marriage Council of Philadelphia,
3828 Locust St., Philadelphia 4, Pa.

Sex Knowledge Inventory, Form X and Form Y. Family Life
Publications Inc., Box 6725, College Station, Durham, N.C.

III. RECOMMENDED FOR THE ENGAGED COUPLE

Leland F. Wood and Robert L. Dickinson, M.D. *Harmony in
Marriage.* Roundtable Press, revised, 1960.

Lewin and Gilmore. *Sex Without Fear.* Family Life Publications
Inc. Box 6725, College Station, Durham, N.C.

Theodore Bovet. *A Handbook to Marriage.* New York: Dolphin
Books, Doubleday and Company, 1960.

George W. Brown. *Your First Week Together.* New York:
National Council of the Churches of Christ in the U.S.A., 1953.

John Coburn. *Prayer and Personal Religion.* Philadelphia: The
Westminster Press, 1957.

Notes

Chapter 1

1. Elizabeth O'Connor, *Call to Commitment*, The story of the Church of the Saviour, Washington, D.C. (New York: Harper & Row, 1963).
2. J. H. Oldham, *Florence Allshorn and the Story of St. Julian's Community* (London: SCM Press, 1951), p. 89.
3. Peter Berger, *The Noise of Solemn Assemblies* (Garden City, N.Y.: Doubleday and Company, 1961). Gibson Winter, *The Suburban Captivity of the Churches*, (Garden City, N. Y.: Doubleday and Company, 1961).
4. C. Wright Mills, *The Causes of World War Three* (New York: Ballantine Books, 1960), p. 166.
5. J. H. Oldham, *Renovatio*, Supplement to Christian Newsletter #320.
6. W. A. Visser 't Hooft, *The Renewal of the Church* (London: SCM Press, 1956; American edition, Philadelphia: The Westminster Press, 1957), pp. 68, 69. W. A. Visser 't Hooft is General Secretary of the World Council of Churches.
7. James M. Gustafson, *Treasure in Earthen Vessels* (New York: Harper & Row, 1961), pp. 111, 112.
8. James Brooks, "As Paint Leaves Brush," *Time*, Feb. 8, 1963, p. 55.
9. Oldham, *Florence Allshorn and the Story of St. Julian's Community*, p. 78.
10. *The Notebooks of Florence Allshorn*, selected and arranged by a member of St. Julian's Community (London: SCM Press, 1957), p. 15.
11. William Shakespeare, *Hamlet*, Act V, sc. ii.

Chapter 2

1. J. H. Oldham, *Florence Allshorn and the Story of St. Julian's Community* (London: SCM Press, 1951), p. 87.
2. *Ibid.*, p. 88.
3. Elizabeth O'Connor, *Call to Commitment* (New York: Harper & Row, 1963), p. 108.
4. Study outlines for *koinonia* groups are included in the Appendix.
5. Dietrich Bonhoeffer, *Life Together* (New York: Harper & Row, 1954), p. 122.

Chapter 3

1. Hendrik Kraemer, *A Theology of the Laity* (Philadelphia: The Westminster Press, 1958), p. 175.
2. "Onward Christian Soldiers" by Sabine Baring-Gould (1834-1934).
3. See Elton Trueblood's *The Company of the Committed* (New York: Harper & Row, 1961) for a provocative analysis of the church as an "army."
4. New York: The Macmillan Company, 1962, pp. 206-10.
5. Dietrich Bonhoeffer, *The Cost of Discipleship* (New York: The Macmillan Company, 1949), pp. 38-39.

6. *Ibid.*

7. William Lazareth, from a lecture, "The Church's Faithful Inreach," presented at the Joint Assembly of the Divisions of Home and Foreign Missions, National Council of the Churches of Christ in the U.S.A., December 1959.

8. Refer to the description of such meetings on p. 31 in Chapter 2 For further detail see a complete outline of these meetings in Robert A. Raines, *New Life in the Church* (New York: Harper & Row, 1961), pp. 111-21.

9. New York: Charles Scribner's Sons, 1962.

10. The story of one such venture is related in Chapter 7; an outline for discussion groups in the job context is to be found in Appendix 2.

11. *The Kingdom of Christ* (New York: Seabury Press, n.d.).

12. *The New York Times*, Apr. 4, 1962.

13. Trueblood, *op. cit.*, p. 97.

14. See Charles M. Wetzel, "First Methodist Sponsors Arts Festival," *Church Management*, August, 1963, Vol. 39, No. 11, p. 9.

15. Elizabeth O'Connor, *Call to Commitment* (New York: Harper & Row, 1963), p. 108.

16 Arthur Higgins and Chester Miller, "Ecumenicity—On the Community Level," *Yale University Divinity News*, March, 1963, p. 3.

Chapter 4

1. Robert McAfee Brown, *The Bible Speaks to You* (Philadelphia: The Westminster Press, 1955).

2. Persons interested in communicating with Outpost leaders can write to The Outpost, 4220 Lee Road, Cleveland 28, Ohio.

3. George W. Webber, *God's Colony in Man's World* (Nashville: Abingdon Press, 1960).

4. Garden City, N. Y.: Doubleday and Company, 1961.

Chapter 5

1. William Stringfellow, *A Private and Public Faith* (Grand Rapids, Mich.: Wm. B. Eerdmans Publishing Company, 1962), pp. 54, 55.

Chapter 6

1. John Wesley's *Journal, abridged by Percy L. Parker* (London: Nisbet and Company, Ltd., 1902), p. 43.

2. "Beneath the Cross of Jesus," by Elizabeth C. Clephane (1830-1869).

Chapter 7

1. R. L. Stevenson, *Vailima Letters* (New York: Charles Scribner's Sons, 1925), p. 16.

2. J. W. Stevenson, *God in My Unbelief* (London: Wm. Collins Sons, Ltd., 1960), p. 16.

3. Paul Tournier, *Guilt and Grace* (New York: Harper & Row, 1962), p. 77.

4. New York: Random House, 1958.

5. The list of readings and questions for discussion for the nine meetings is in the Appendix.

6. By Robert Calhoun (New York: Association Press, 1943).

7. Paul Tournier, *The Meaning of Persons* (New York: Harper & Row, 1957), pp. 181, 184, 185.

8. By Benjamin R. Epstein and Arnold Foster (New York: Farrar, Straus and Cudahy, 1962).

9. "The Country Club an American Idyl," *Life*, Aug. 3, 1962, Vol. 53, p. 58.

Chapter 8

1. Margaret T. Applegarth, *Moment by Moment* (New York: Harper & Row, 1955), p. 5.

2. "Ode on a Grecian Urn."

3. J. H. Oldham, *Florence Allshorn and the Story of St. Julian's Community*, (London: SCM Press, 1959), p. 69.

4. Martin Luther, *Three Treatises* translated by W. A. Lambert (Philadelphia: Muhlenberg Press, 1947), p. 251.

5. *Ibid.*, pp. 277-79.

6. William Russell Maltby, *Obiter Scripta* (London: The Epworth Press, 1952), p. 153.

7. Jacques Ellul, *The Presence of the Kingdom* (London: SCM Press, 1951), pp. 20-21.

8. Oldham, *op. cit.*, p. 19.

9. John Ciardi, "Manner of Speaking," in *Saturday Review*, Sept. 15, 1962, p. 17.

10. New York: Seabury Press, 1959.

11. E. Herman, *Creative Prayer* (New York: Harper & Row, n.d.), p. 107.

12. Oldham, *op. cit.*, p. 34.

13. Translated by Frederick H. Hedge, 1852.

14. Paul Tournier, *The Meaning of Persons* (New York: Harper & Row, 1957), p. 154.

15. *Ibid.*, p. 31.

16. Oldham, *op. cit.*, p. 21.

Chapter 9

1. William Shakespeare, *Macbeth*, Act V, sc. v.

2. Calvin Kytle, "Cracks in the Cornucopia," in *Saturday Review*, Aug. 27, 1960, p. 11.

3. Shakespeare, *King Lear*, Act III, sc. ii.

4. T. S. Eliot, "The Cocktail Party," in *The Complete Poems and Plays* (New York: Harcourt, Brace and Company, 1952), pp. 362, 364.

5. Phyllis McGinley, "Loafing: A Big Challenge to Men, A Laugh to Wives," in *Life*, Dec. 28, 1959, p. 155.

6. Sloan Wilson, "Happy Idle Hours Become a Ratrace," in *Life*, Dec. 28, 1959, p. 119.

7. Joyce Glassman, *Come and Join the Dance* (New York: Atheneum Publishers, 1961); quoted in a review by Gerald Walker in the *New York Times Book Review*, Jan. 28, 1962, p. 38.

8. T. S. Eliot, "The Hollow Men," in *op. cit.*, p. 59.

9. Teilhard de Chardin, *The Divine Milieu* (New York: Harper & Row, 1960), p. 14.

10. A highly provocative attempt to search out a new shape of theology is made by John A. T. Robinson, in his book *Honest to God* (London: SCM Press, 1963).

11. See Appendix for Bible study outlines.

12. New York: Harper & Row, 1954.

13. Mildred Binns Young, *The Pendle Hill Bulletin* (Wallingford, Pa.), Aug. 1962, No. 161.

14. Edited by Edward J. Klein (New York: Harper & Row, 1943).

15. E. Herman, *Creative Prayer*, (New York: Harper & Row, n.d.), pp. 108-9.

16. "The Gift Outright," *New York Times*, Jan. 15, 1961.

Chapter 10

1. *The Cost of Discipleship* (New York: The Macmillan Company, 1948).

2. Teilhard de Chardin, *The Divine Milieu* (New York: Harper & Row, 1960), pp. 41, 42.

3. Bonhoeffer, *op. cit.*, p. 32.

4. Forbes Robinson, *Letters to His Friends* (London: Spottiswoode and Company, Ltd. 1904), pp. 68, 69.

5. Harper Lee, *To Kill a Mockingbird* (Philadelphia: J. B. Lippincott Company, 1960), p. 105.

6. "A Beaten Family in a Rio Slum," *Life*, June 16, 1961, Vol. 50, p. 86.

7. Random House, 1946, Vintage Books edition, 1958), pp. 191-92.

8. Dietrich Bonhoeffer, *Letters and Papers from Prison*, (London: SCM Press, 1953), p. 185.

9. Elizabeth C. Clephane, "Beneath the Cross of Jesus."

10. Quoted by Gordon Ruopp, *The Righteousness of God* (New York: Philosophical Library, Inc., 1953), p. 190.

11. Matthew Bridges and Godfrey Thring, "Crown Him with Many Crowns."

12. Rev. 19:6, 11:15, 19:16, AV.

Scripture Index

Set in Linotype Janson
Composed, printed and bound by The Haddon Craftsmen, Inc.
HARPER & ROW, PUBLISHERS, INCORPORATED